KEEPING IT LOW KEY

Bass Guitar Tablature Notebook

· Seven 4-Line Staves and 6 Chord Diagrams Per Page ·

· 100 Pages (50 Sheets) of TAB Pages ·

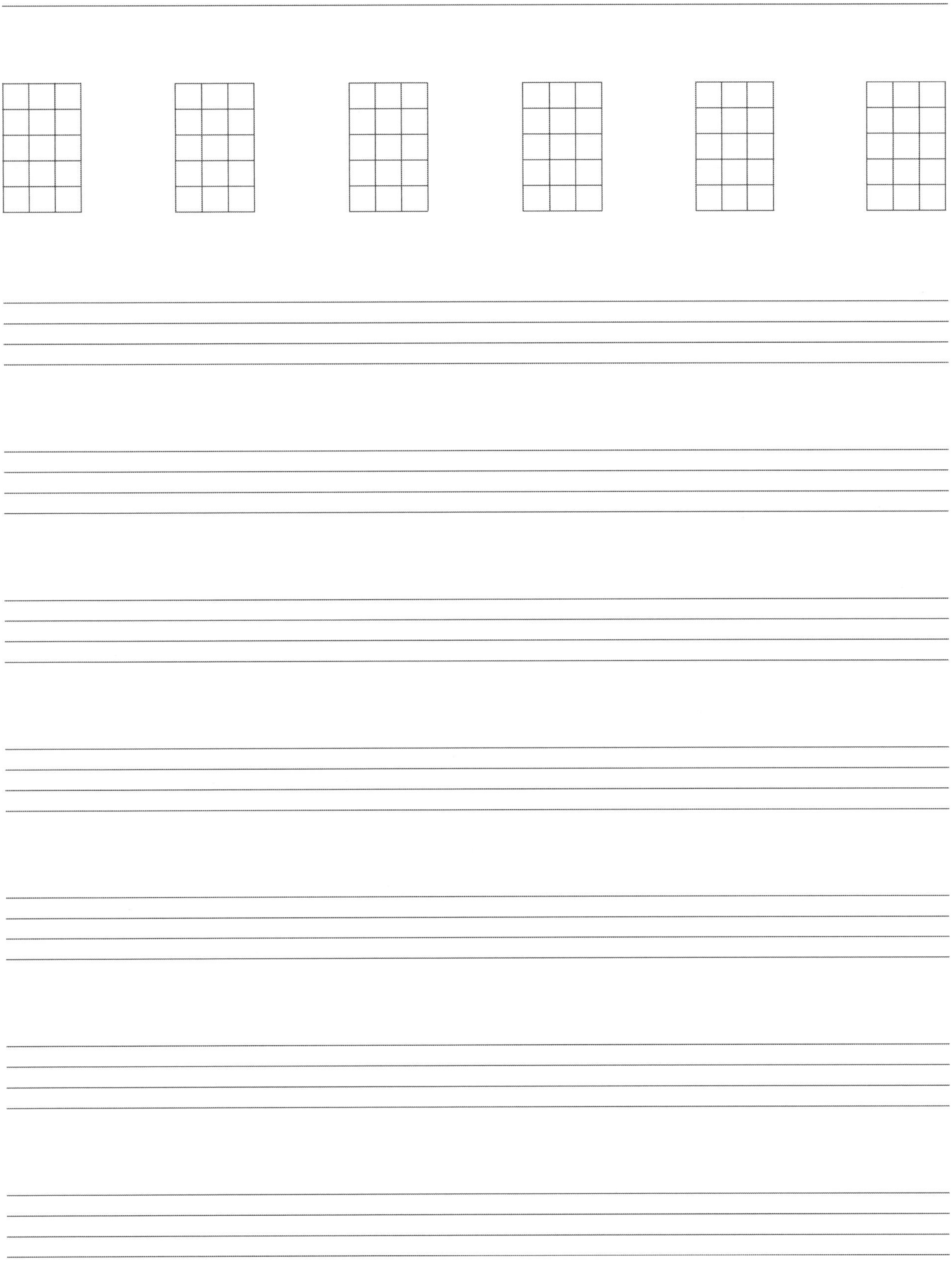

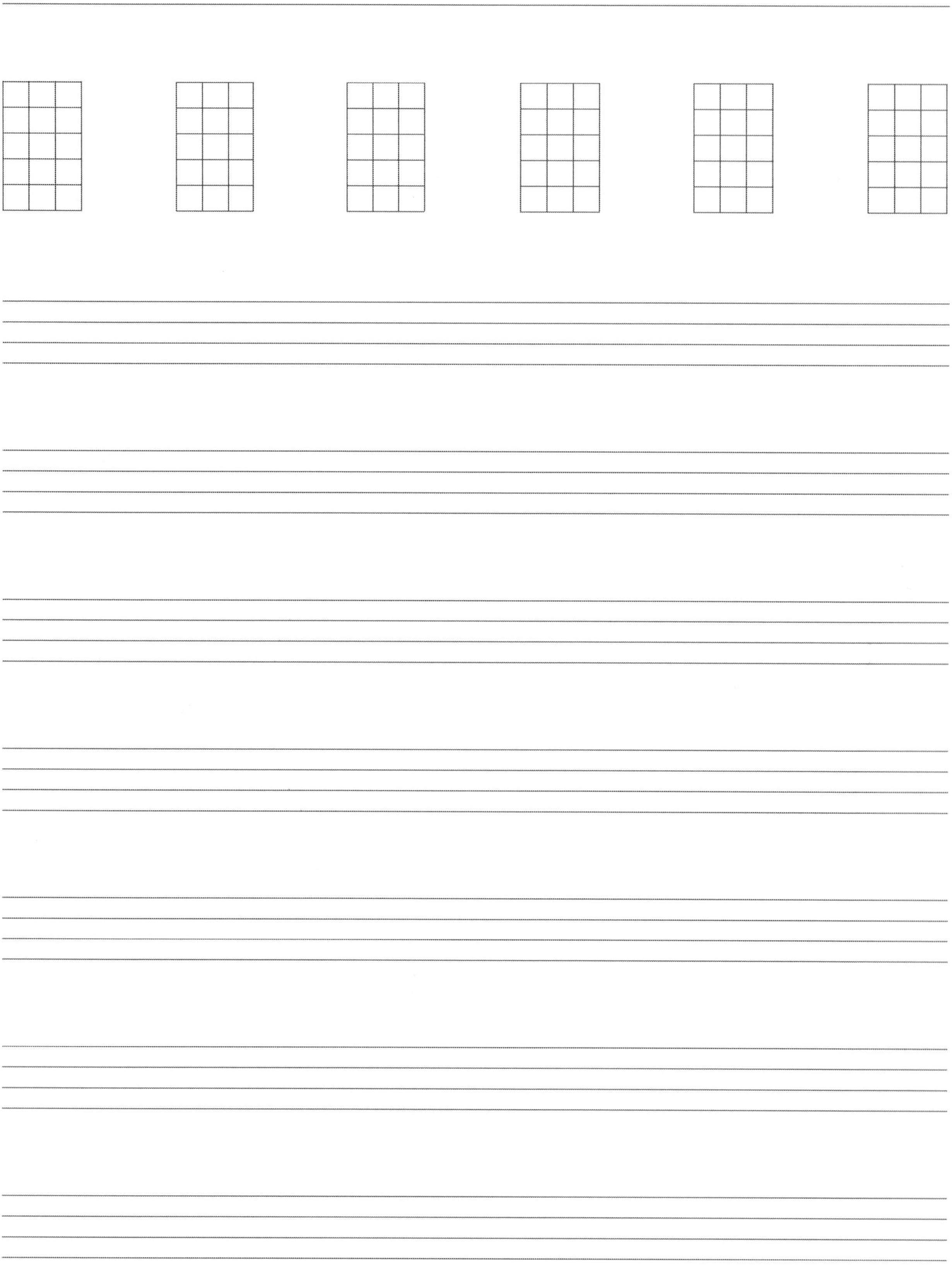

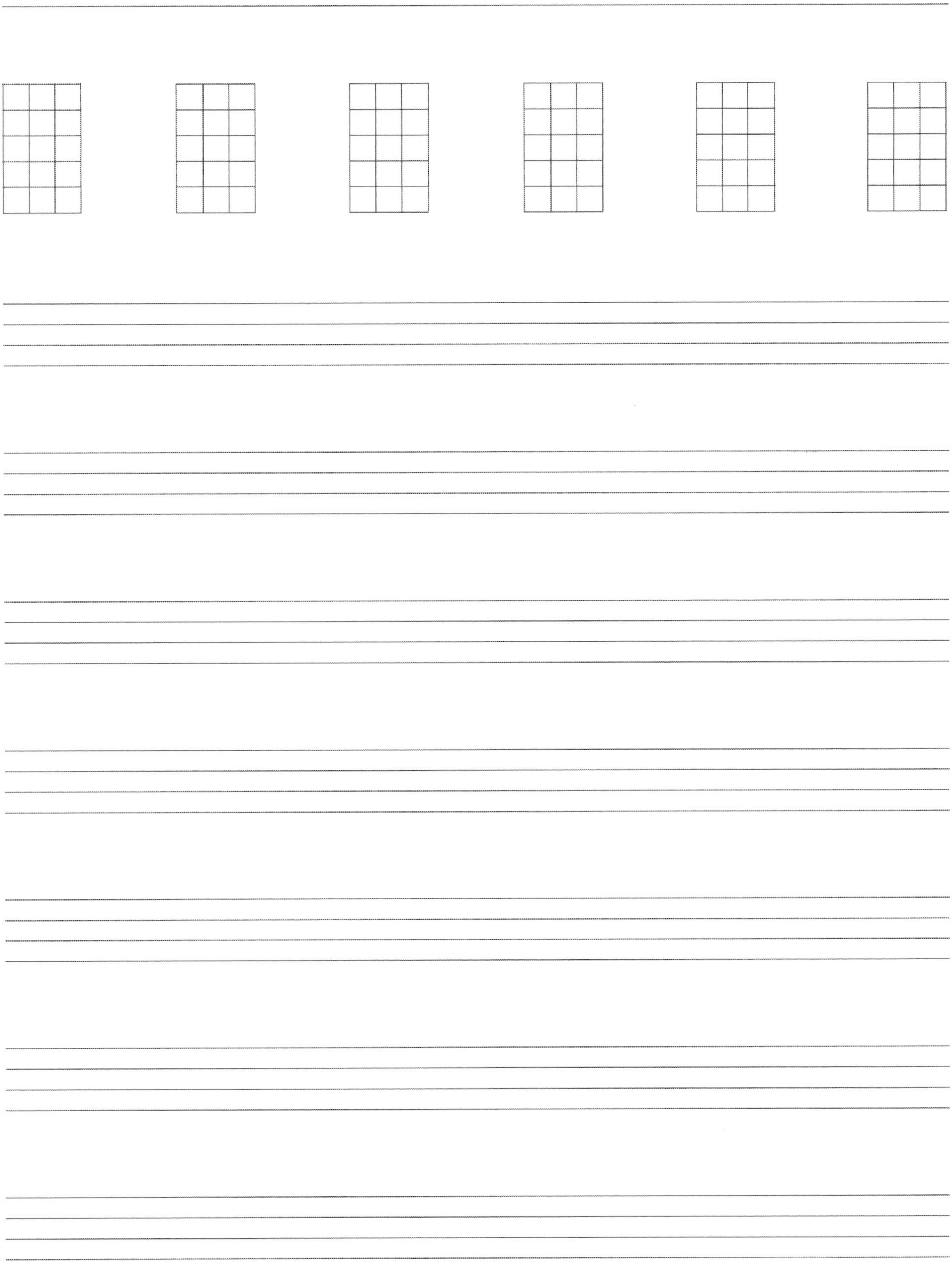

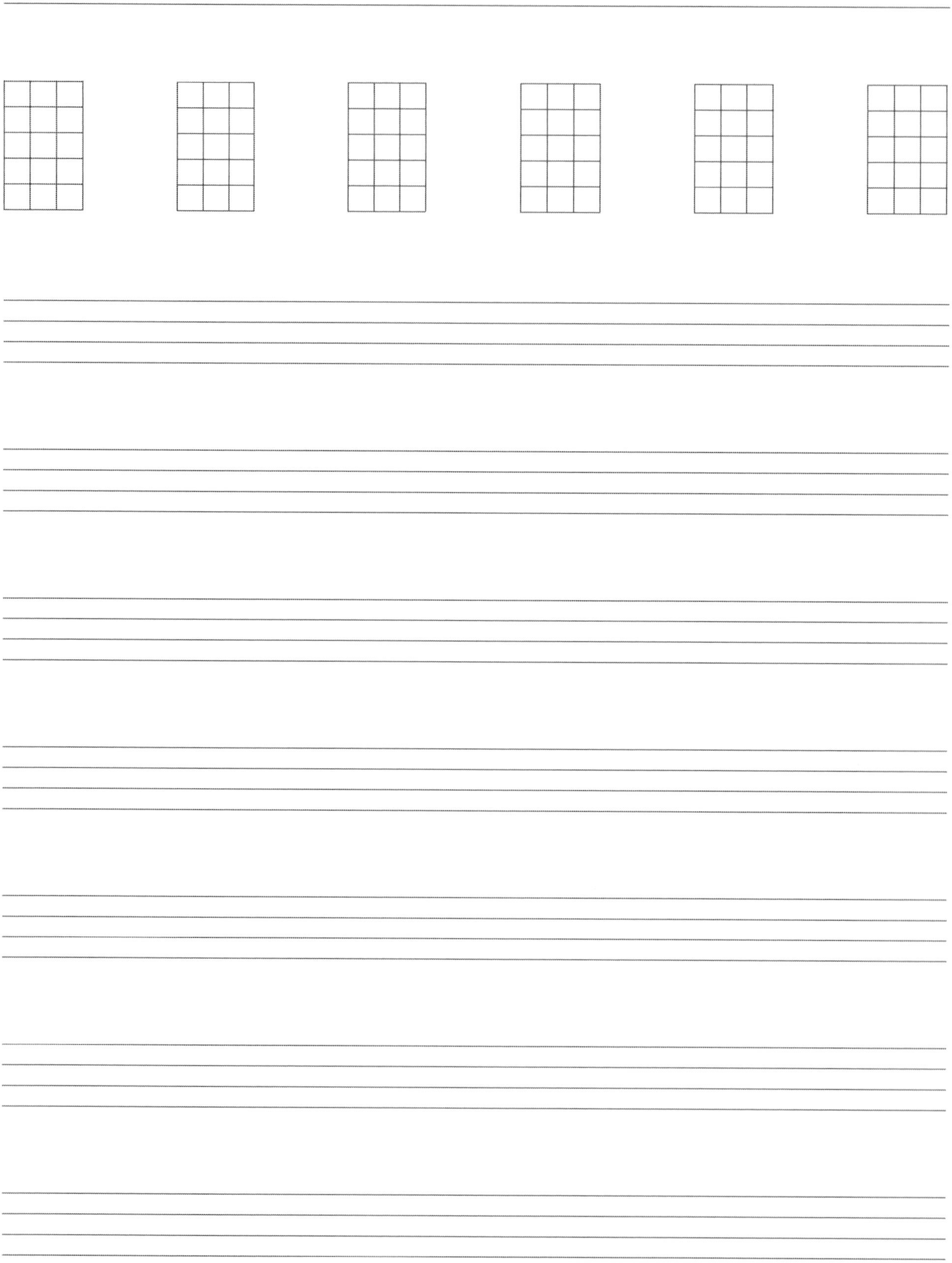

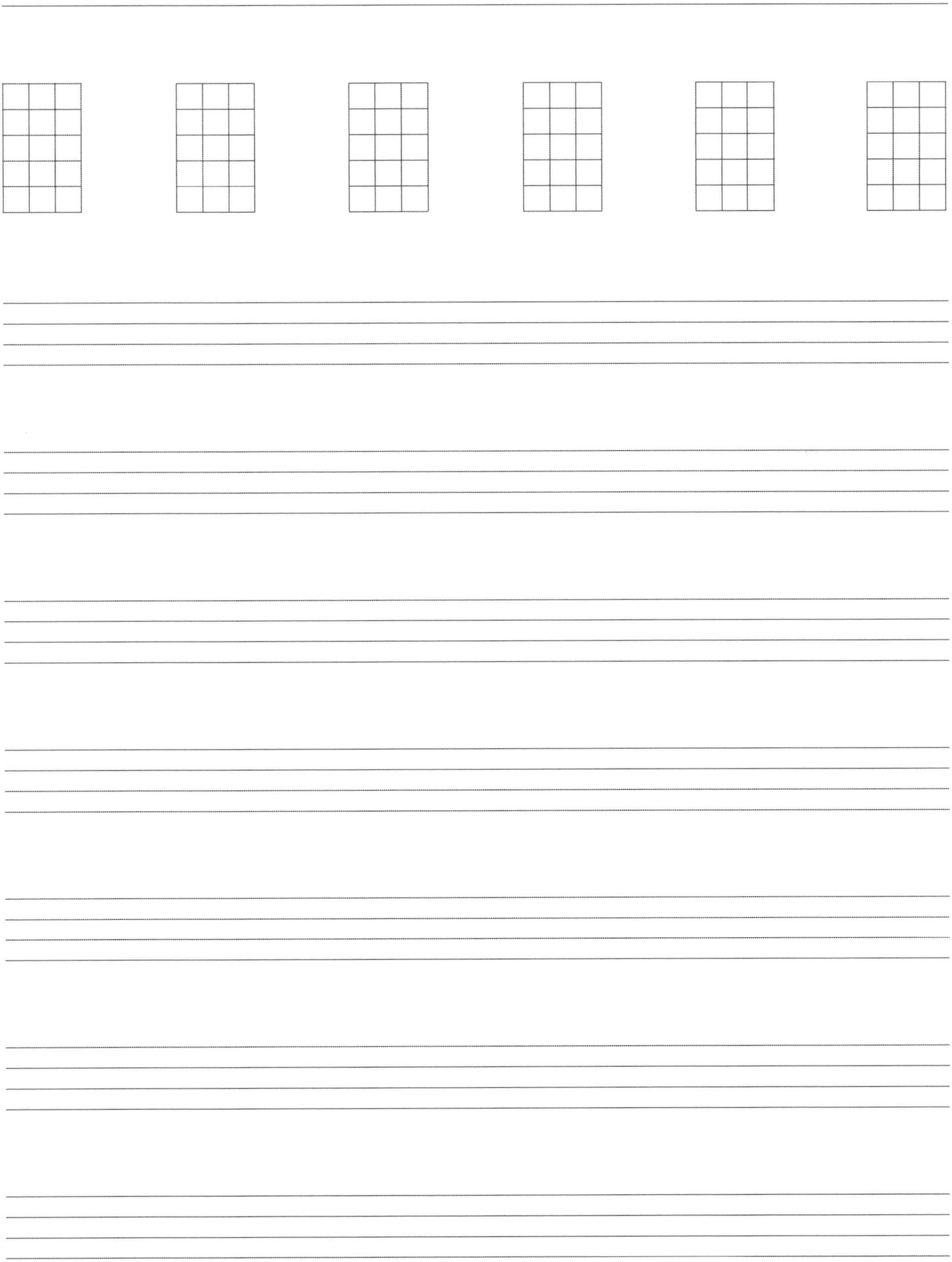

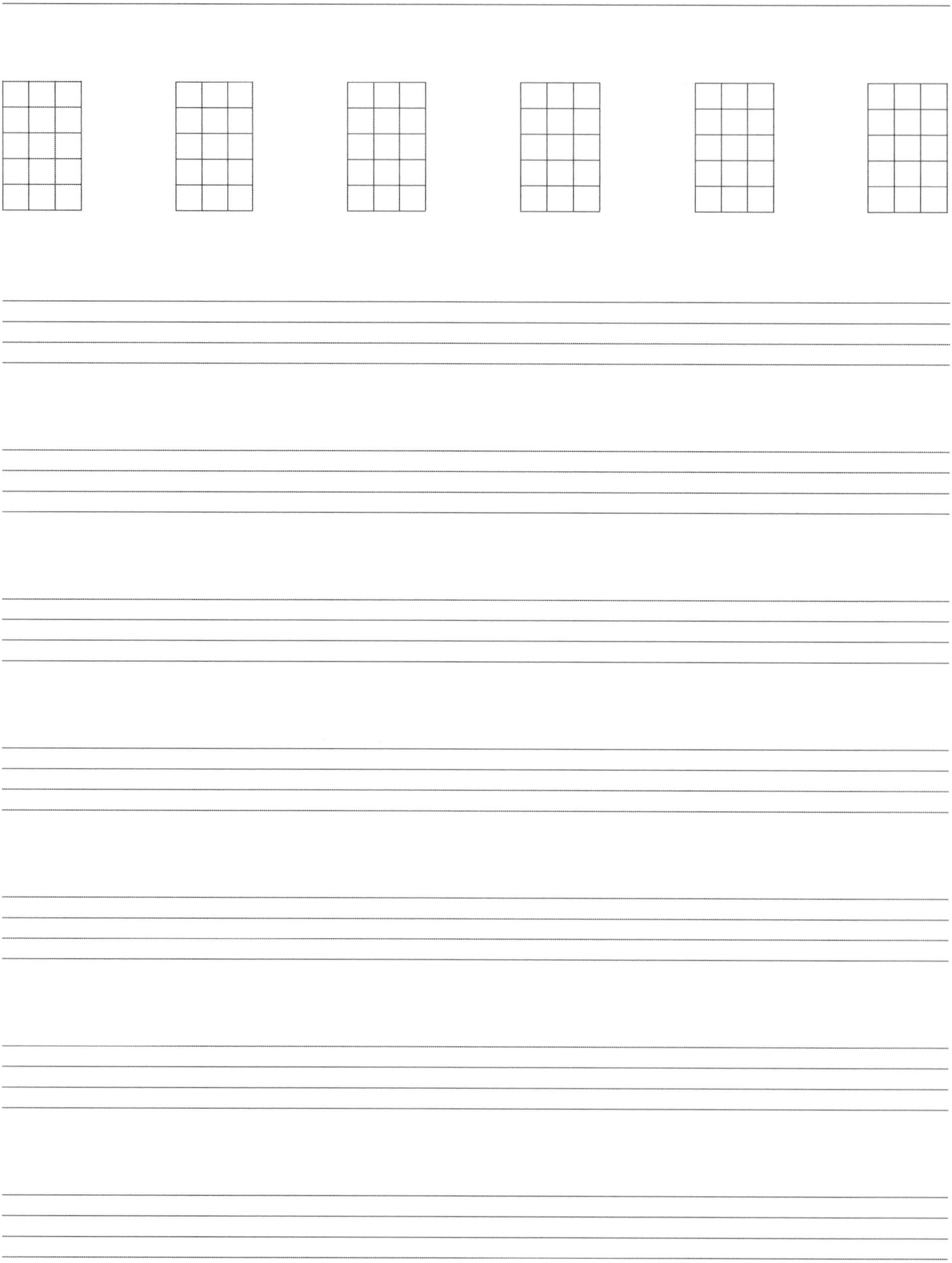

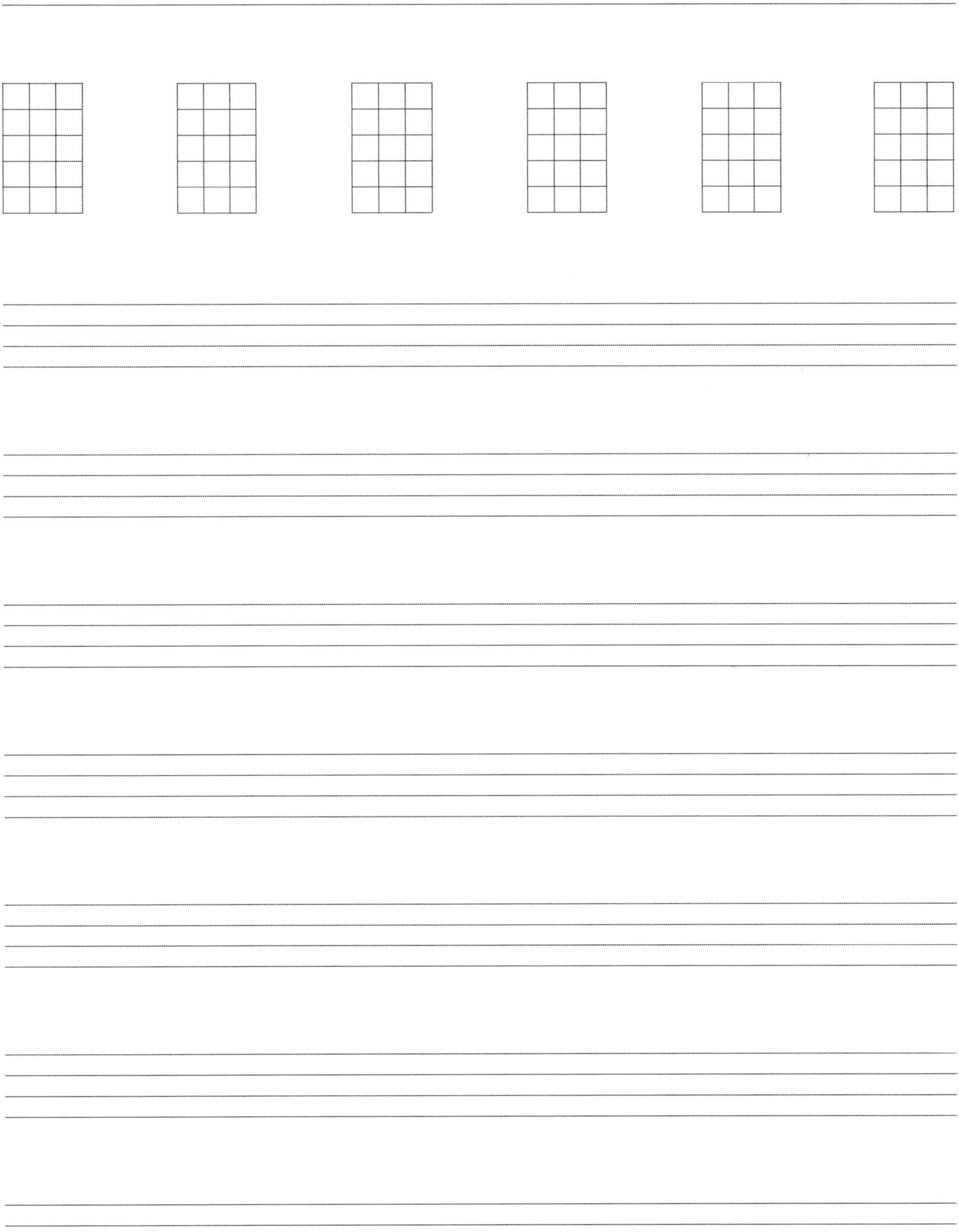

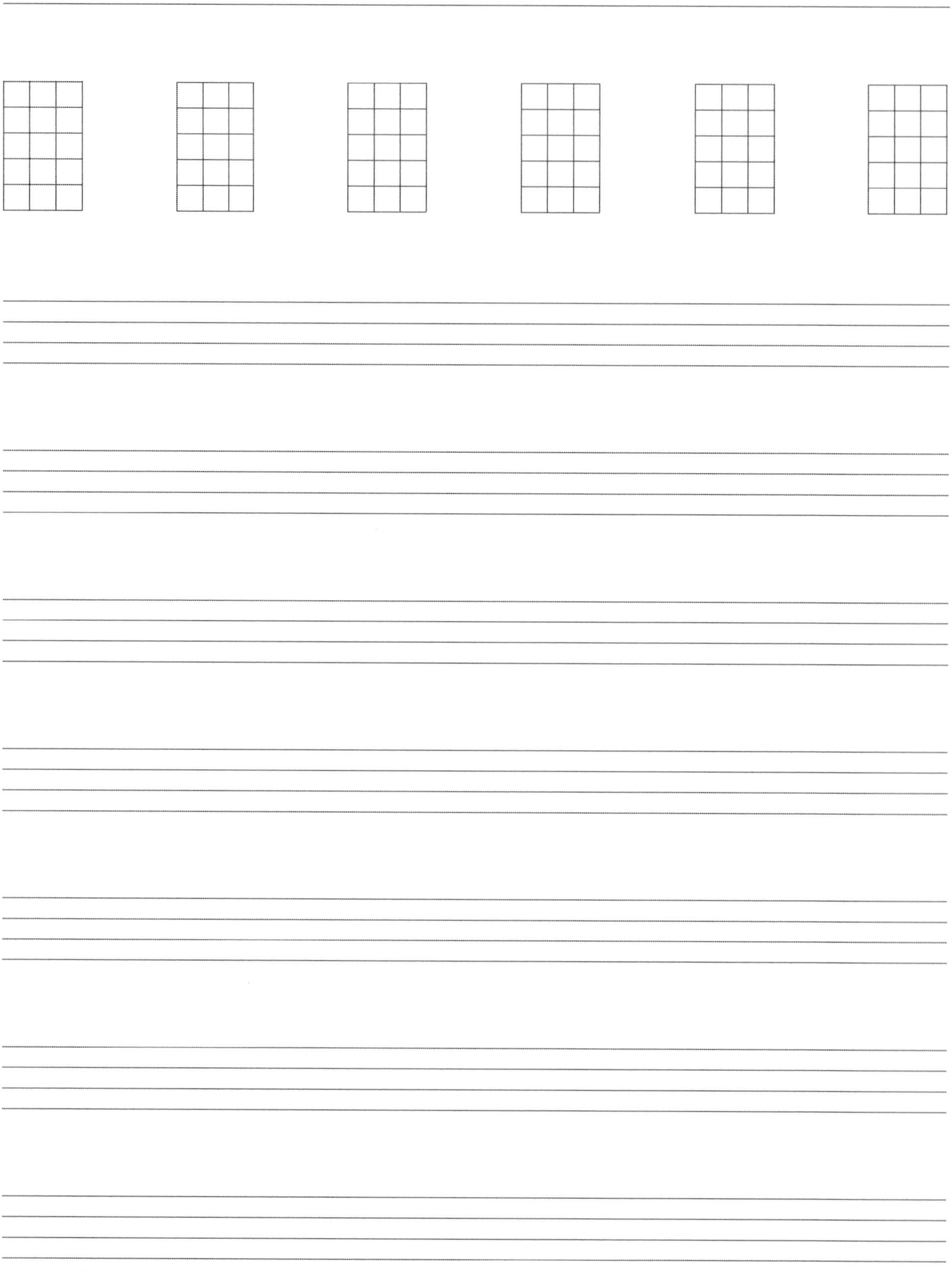

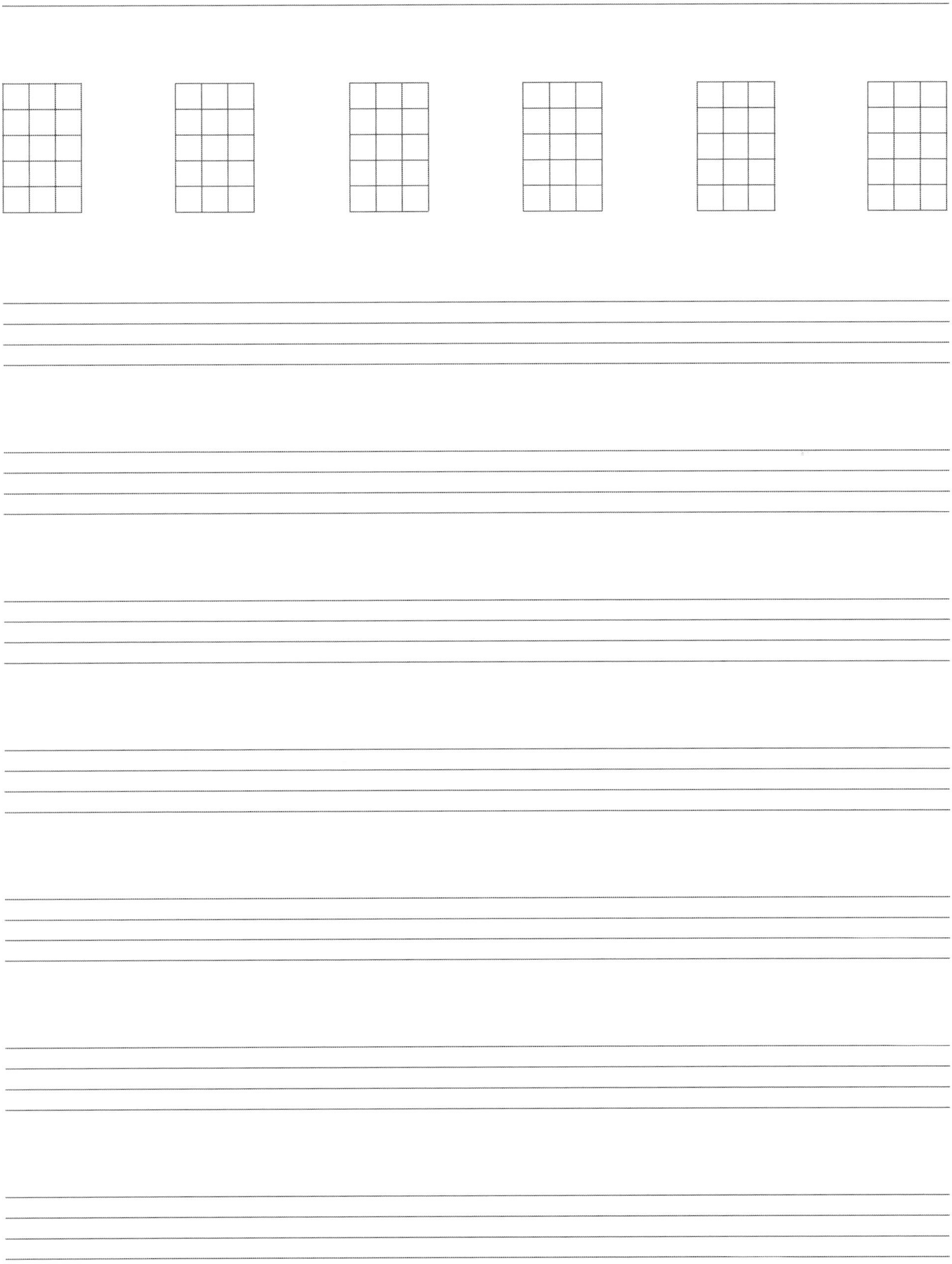

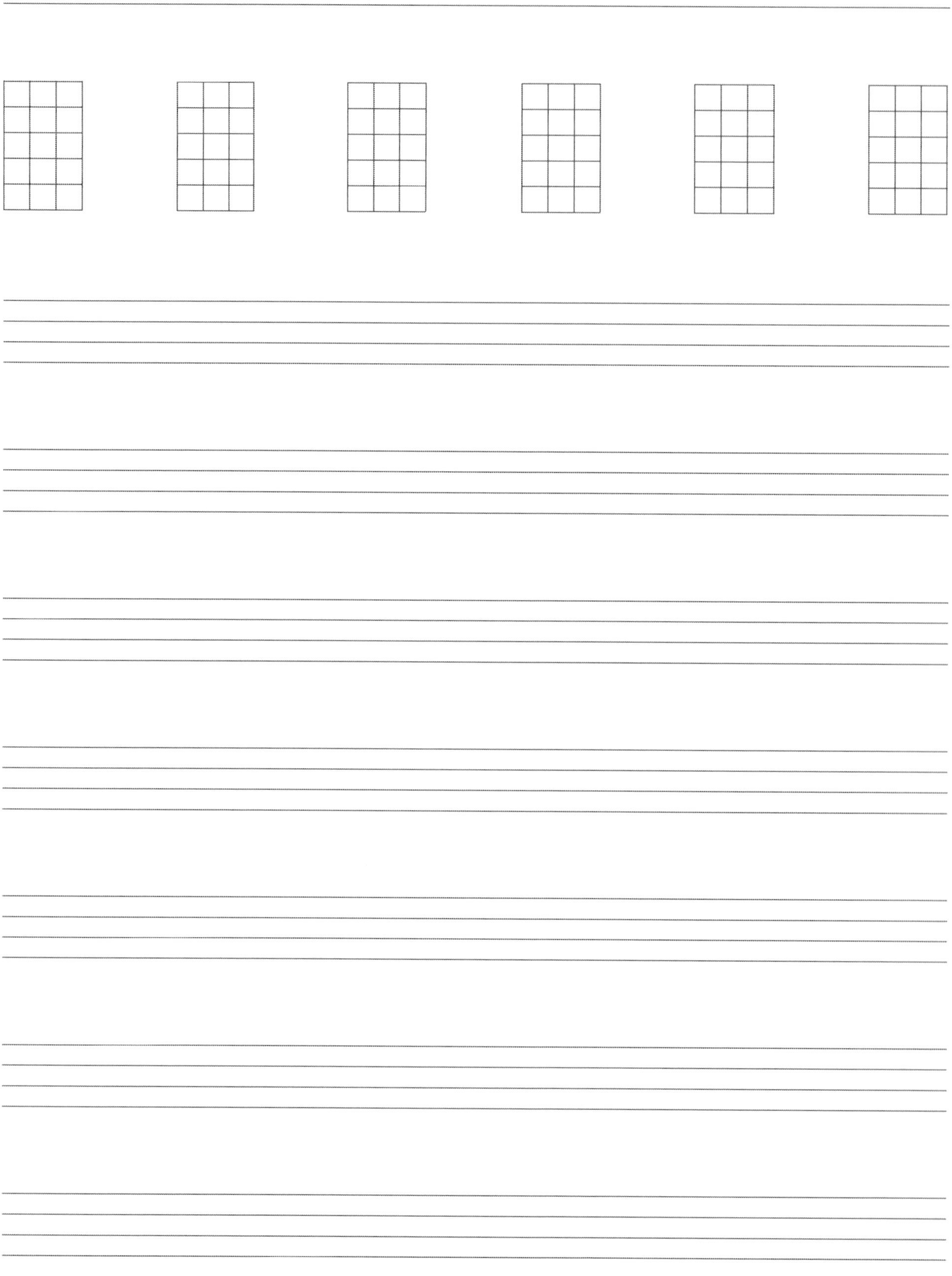

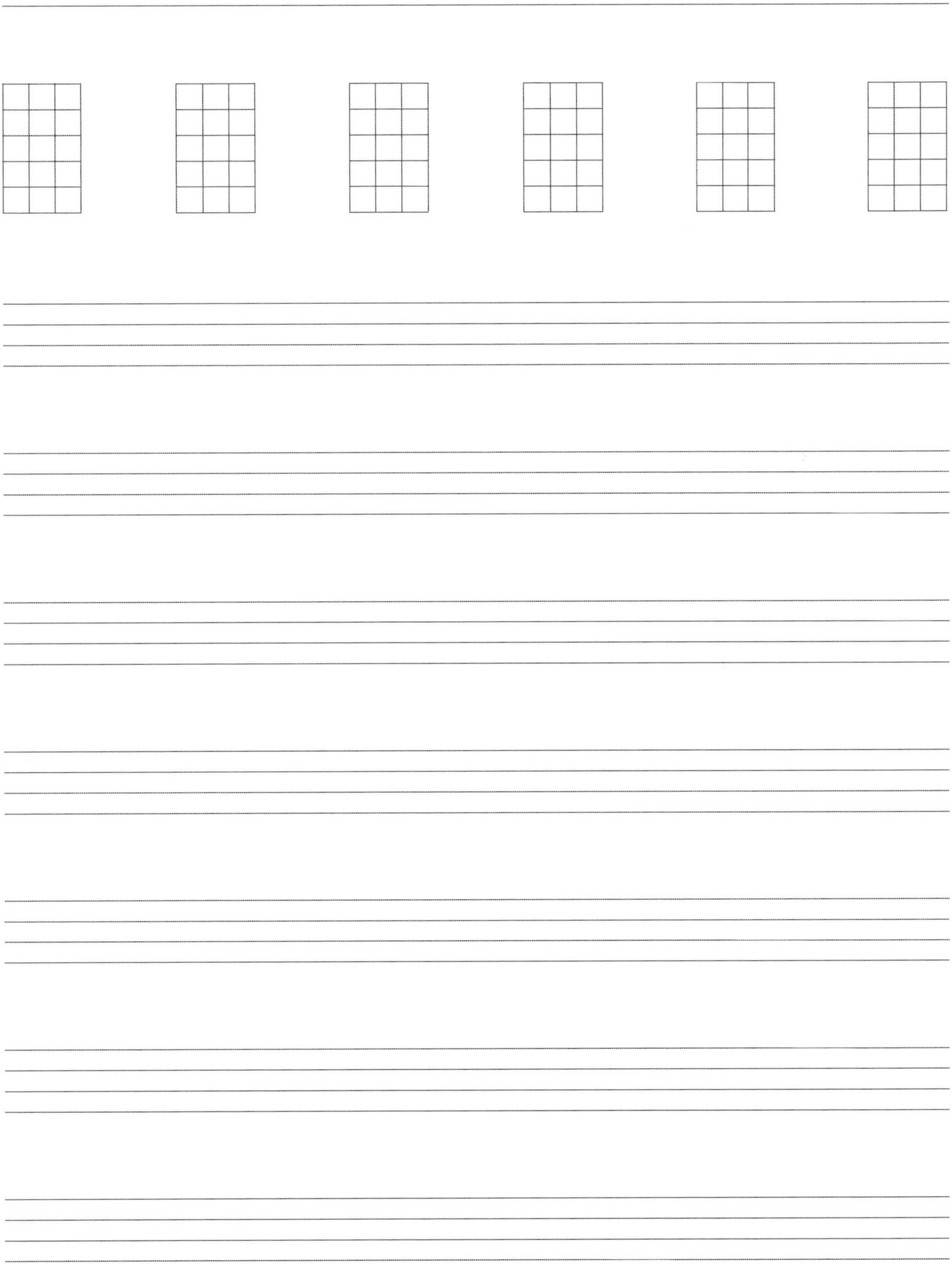

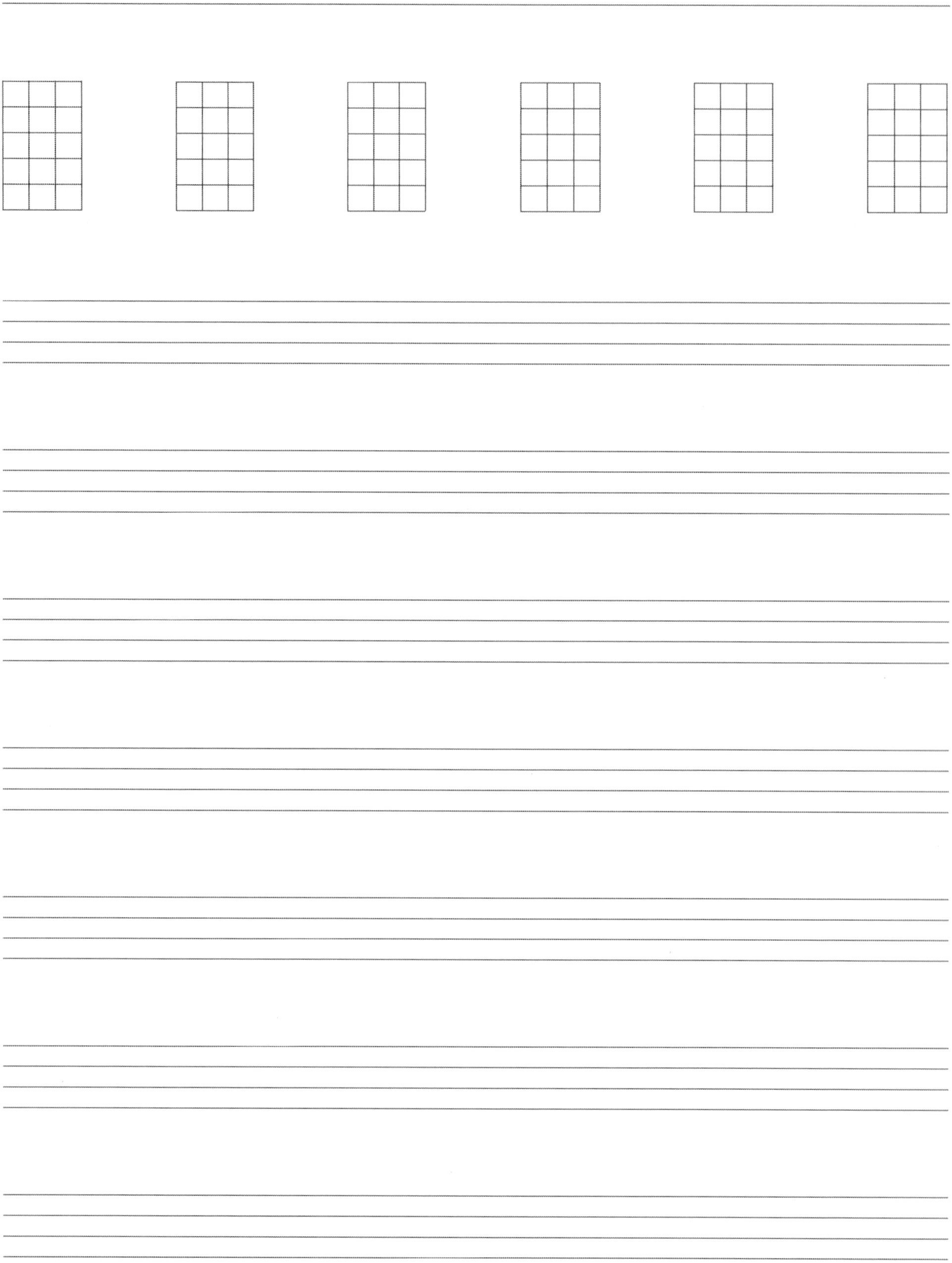

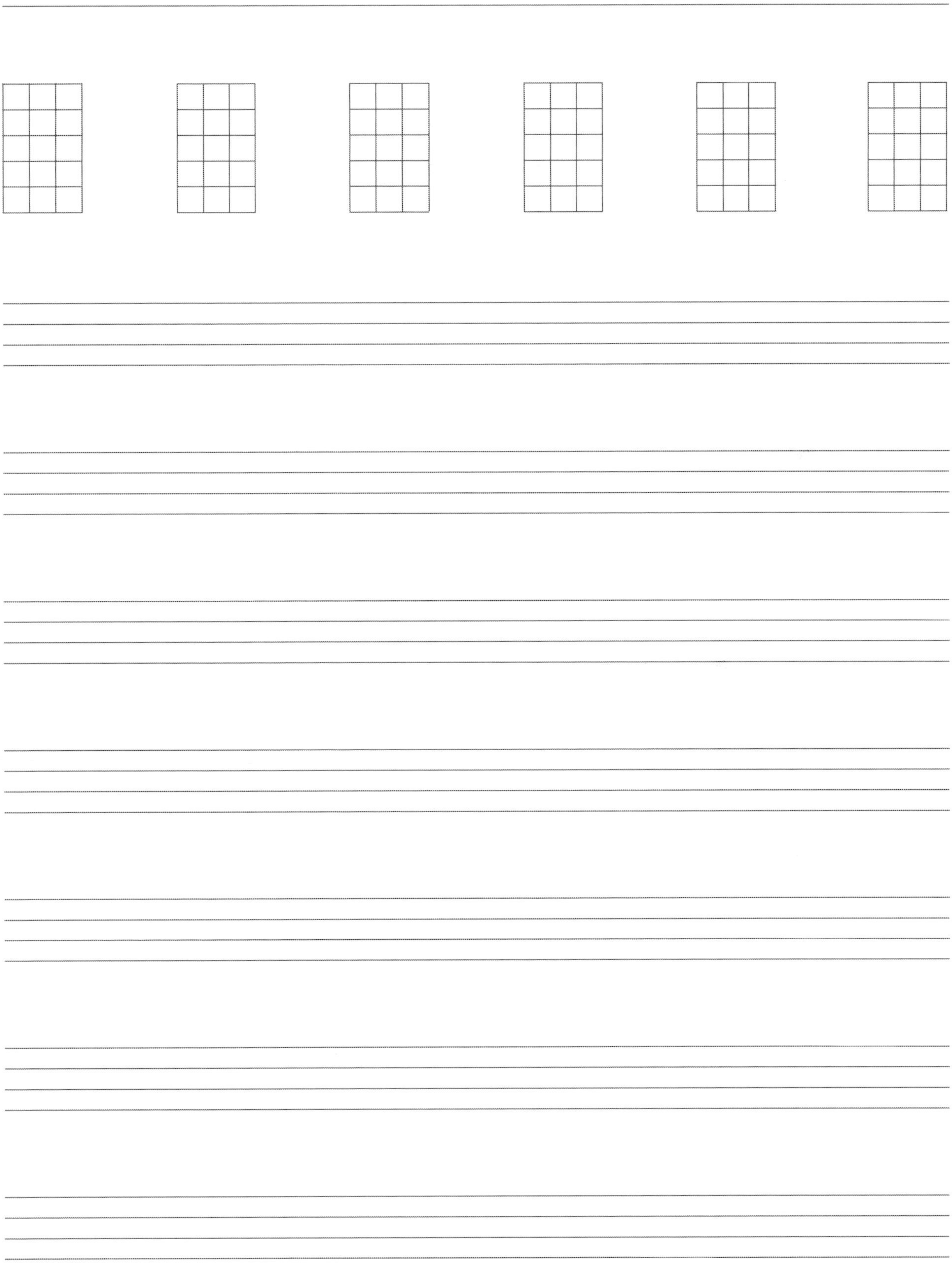

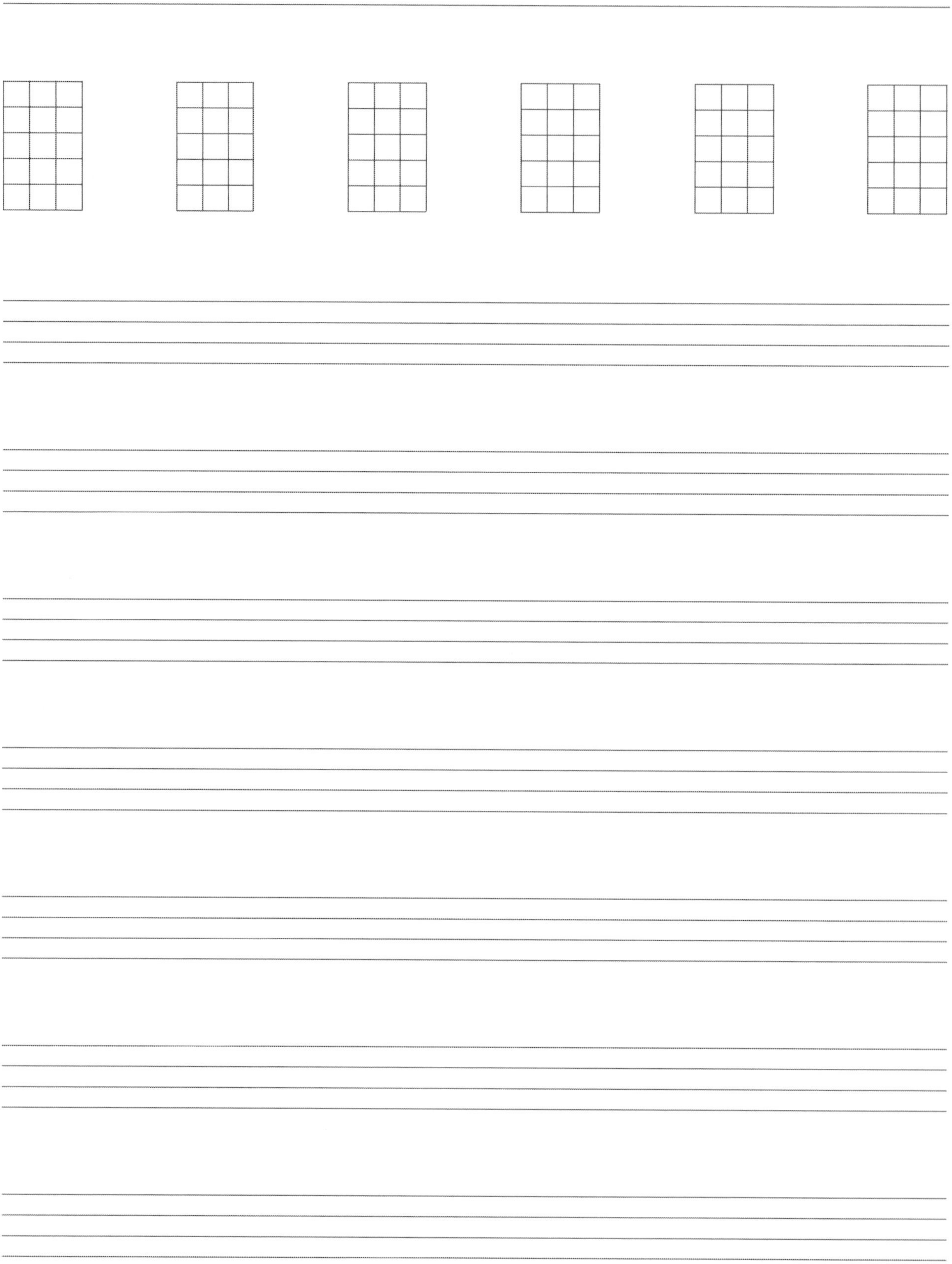

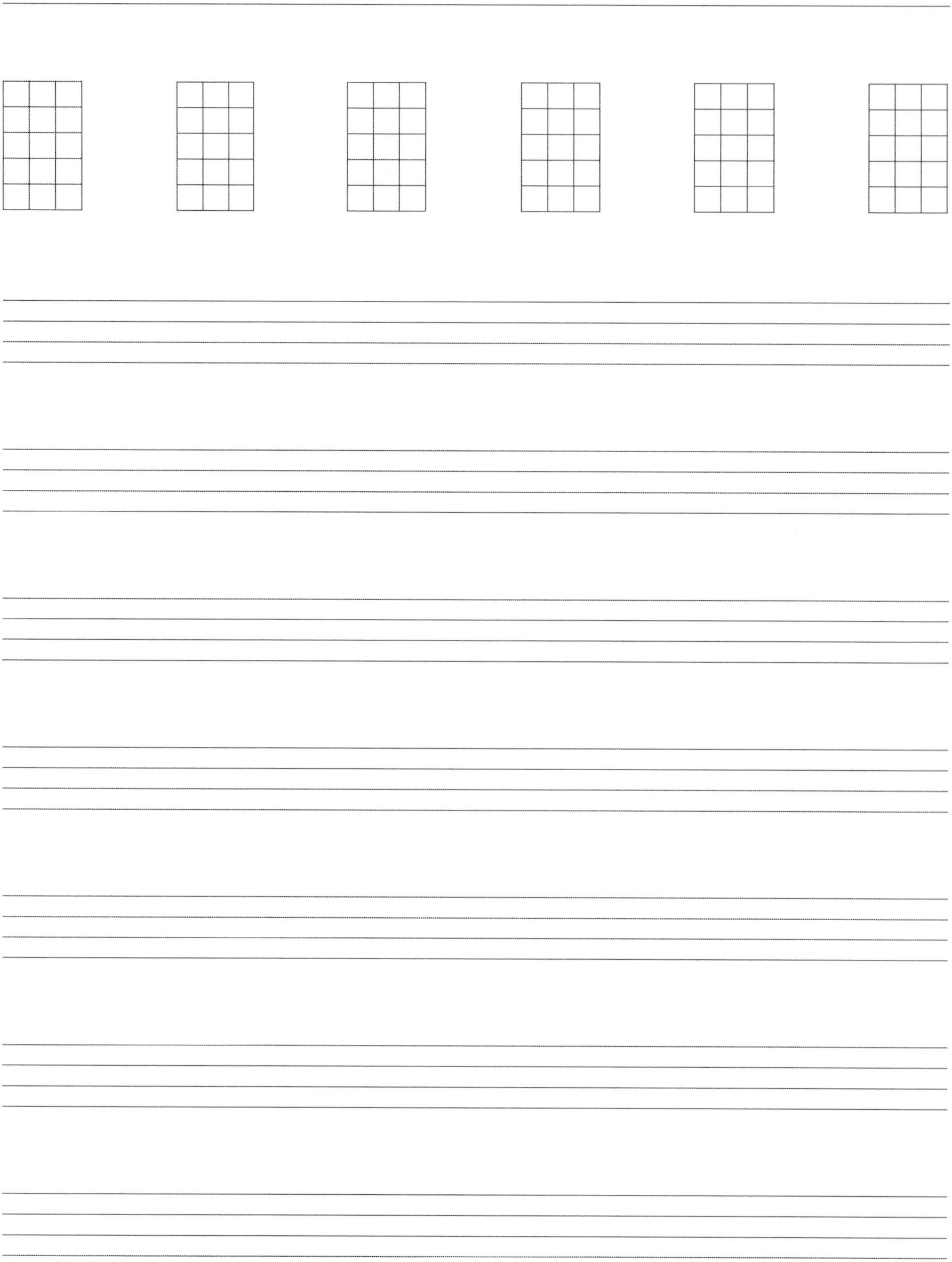

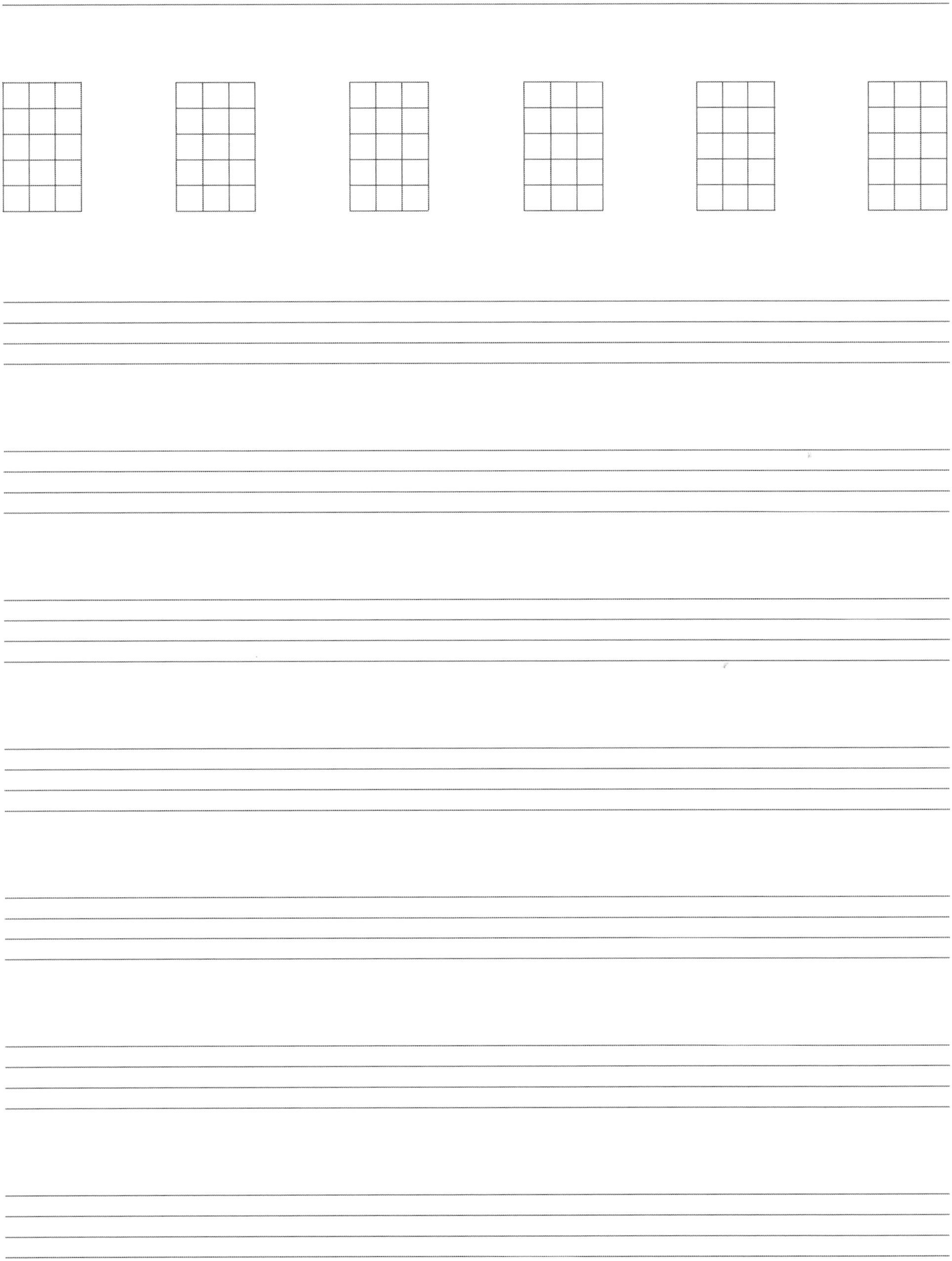

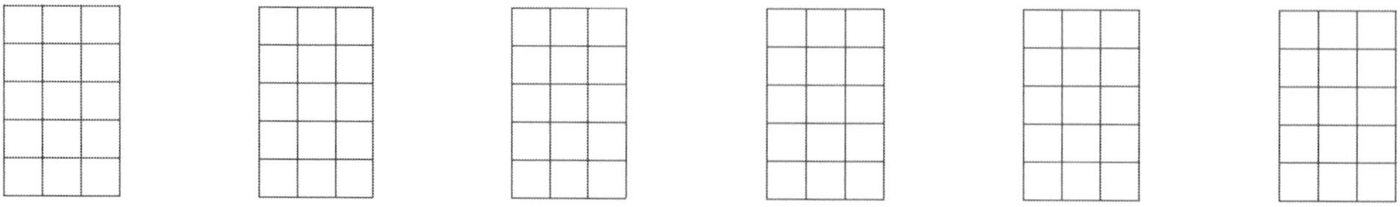

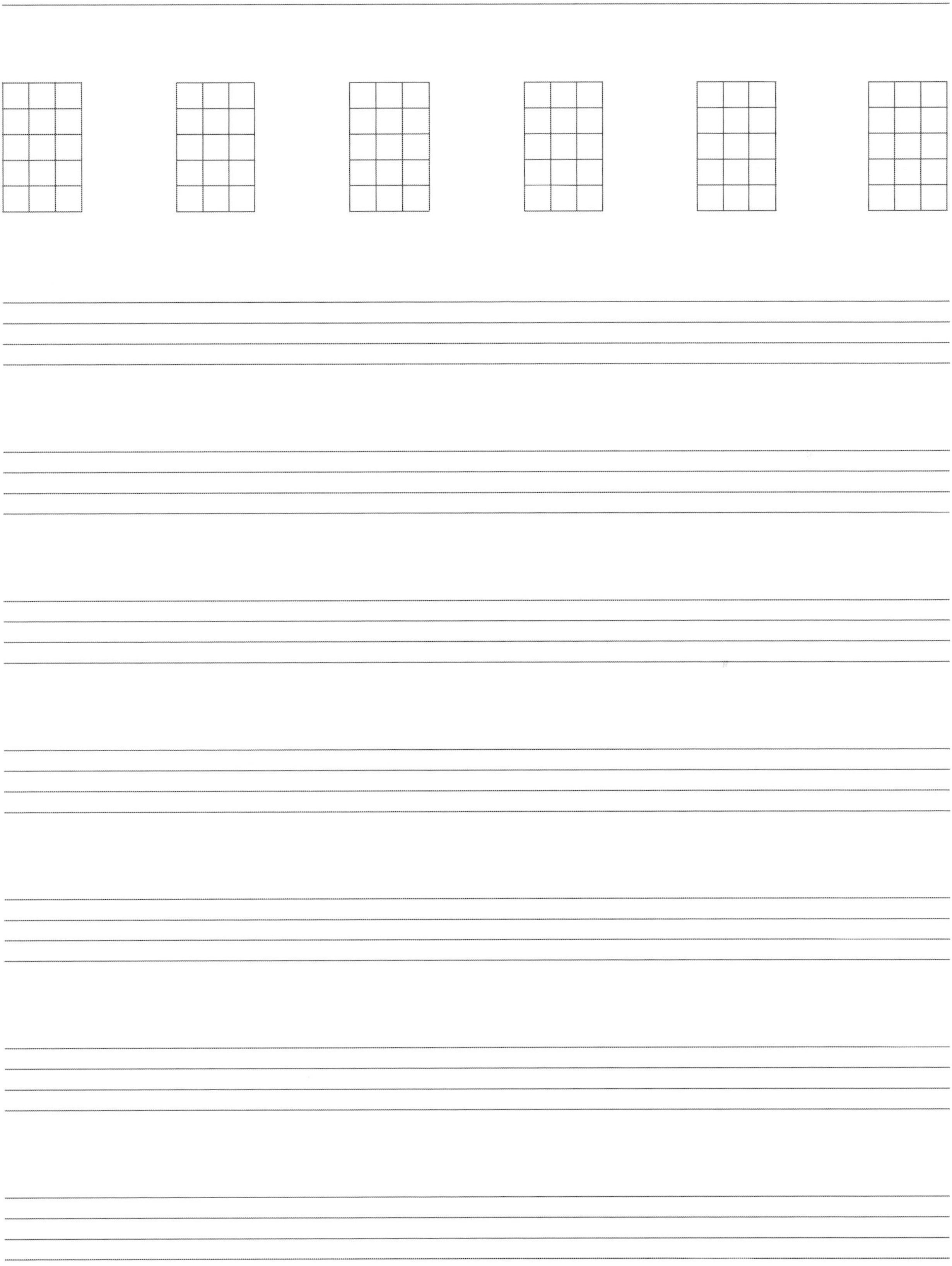

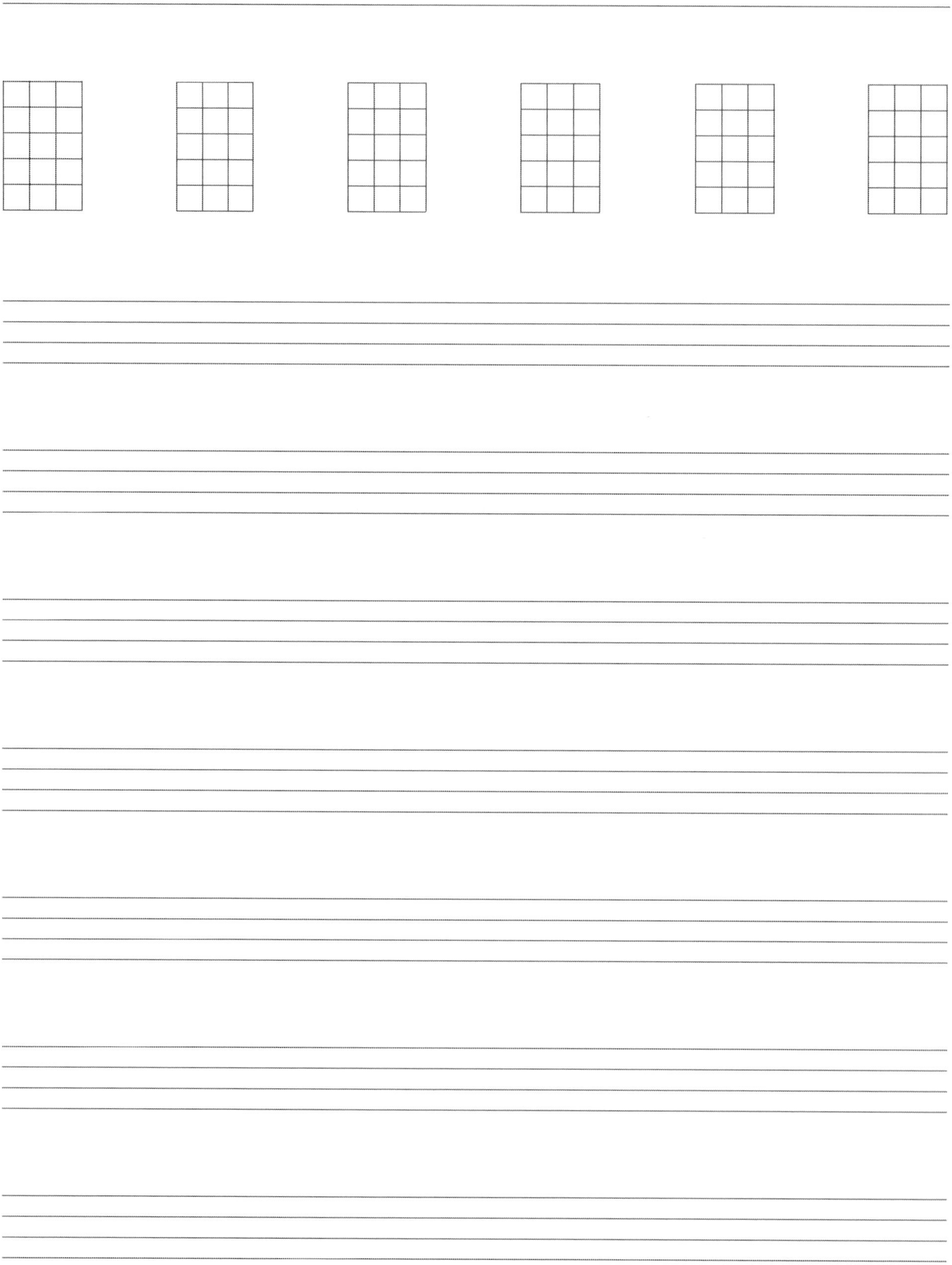

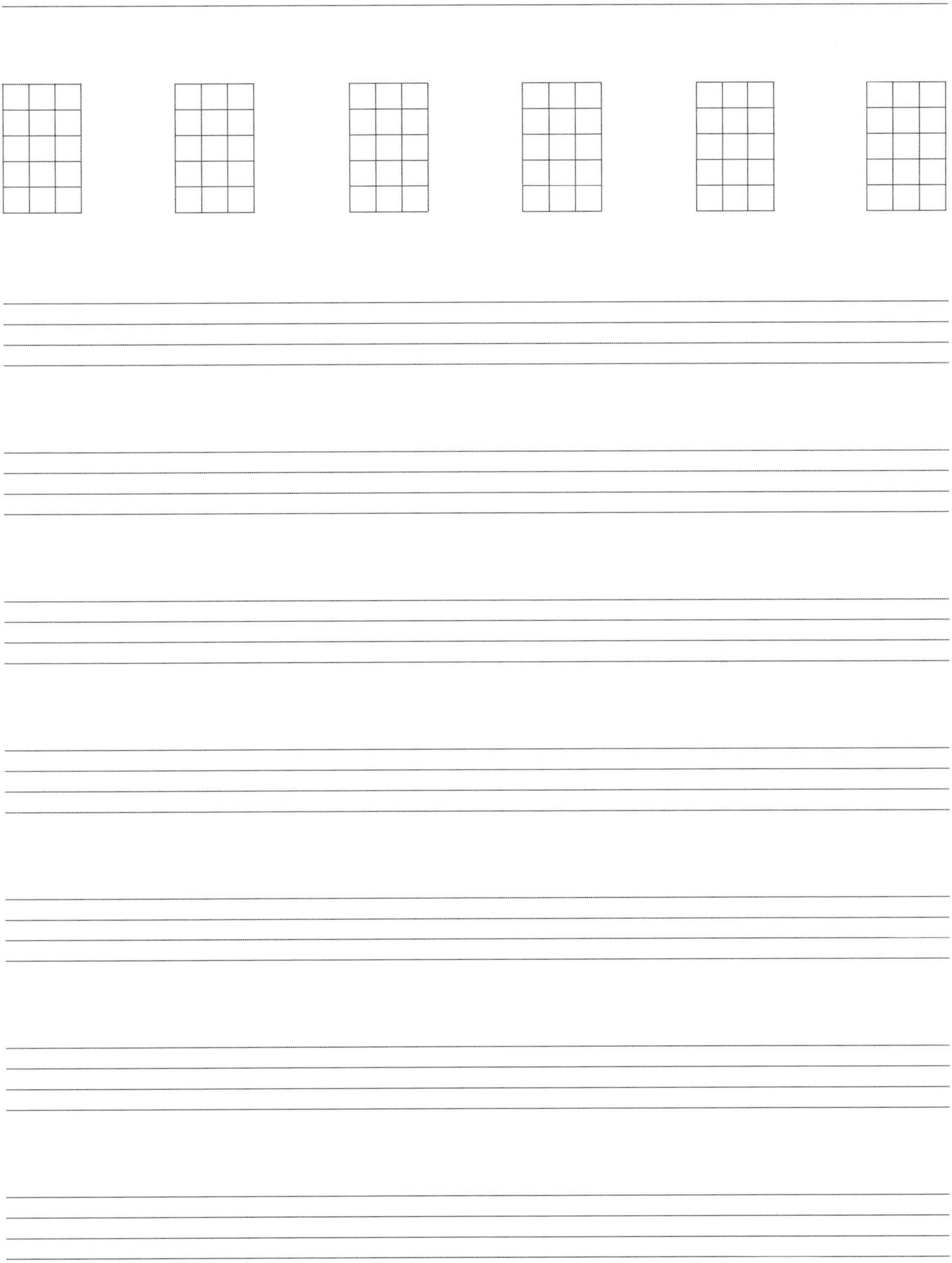

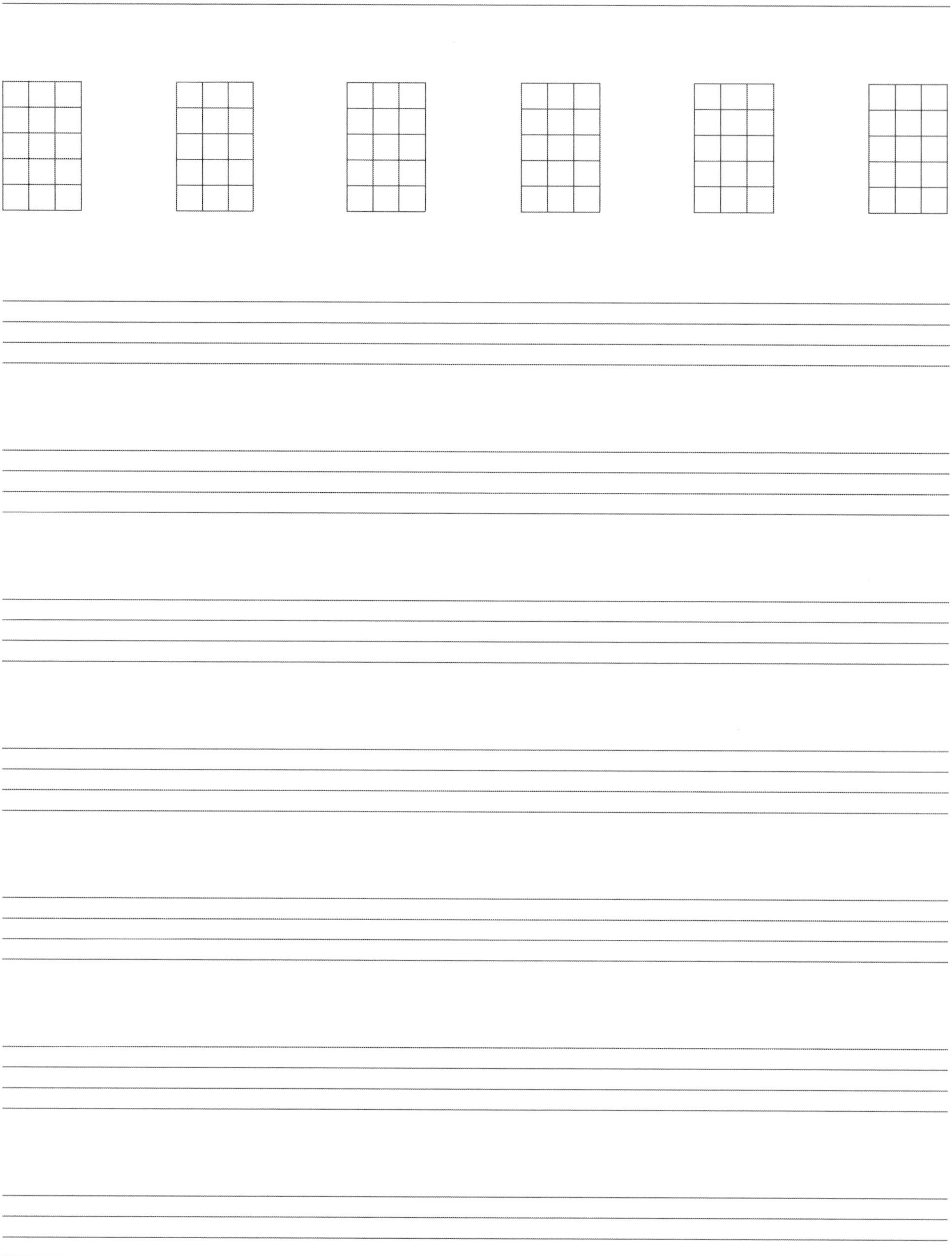

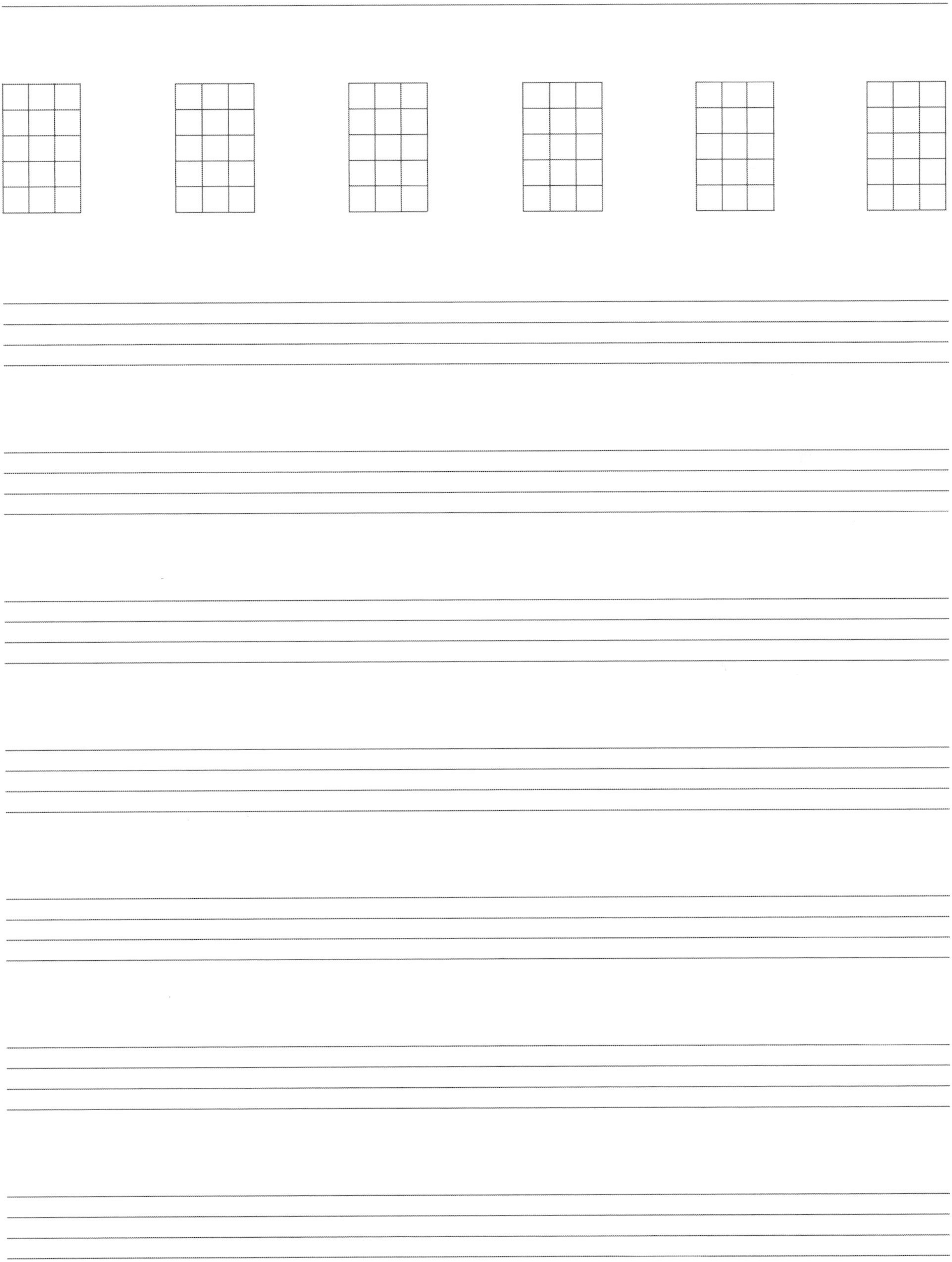

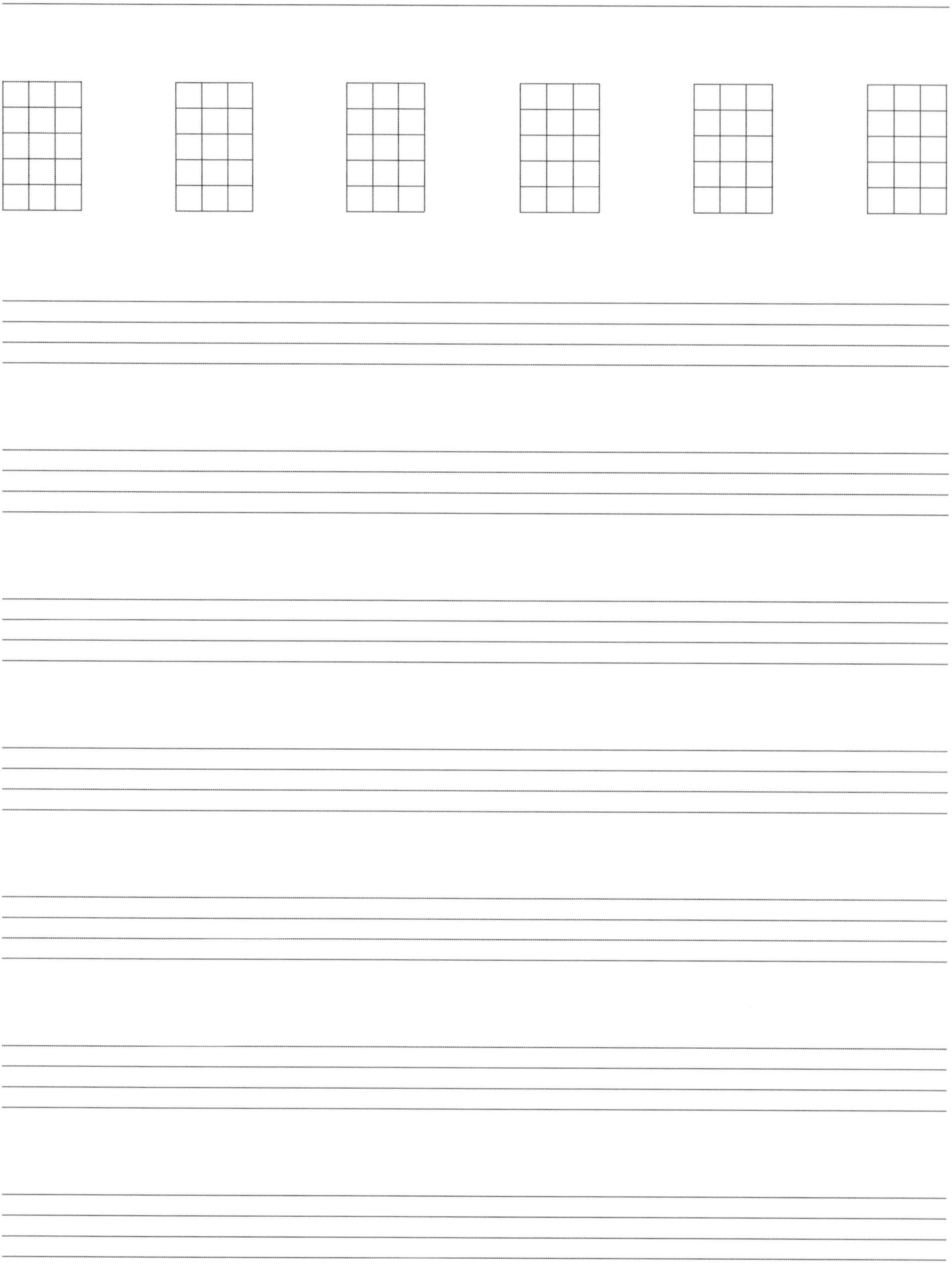

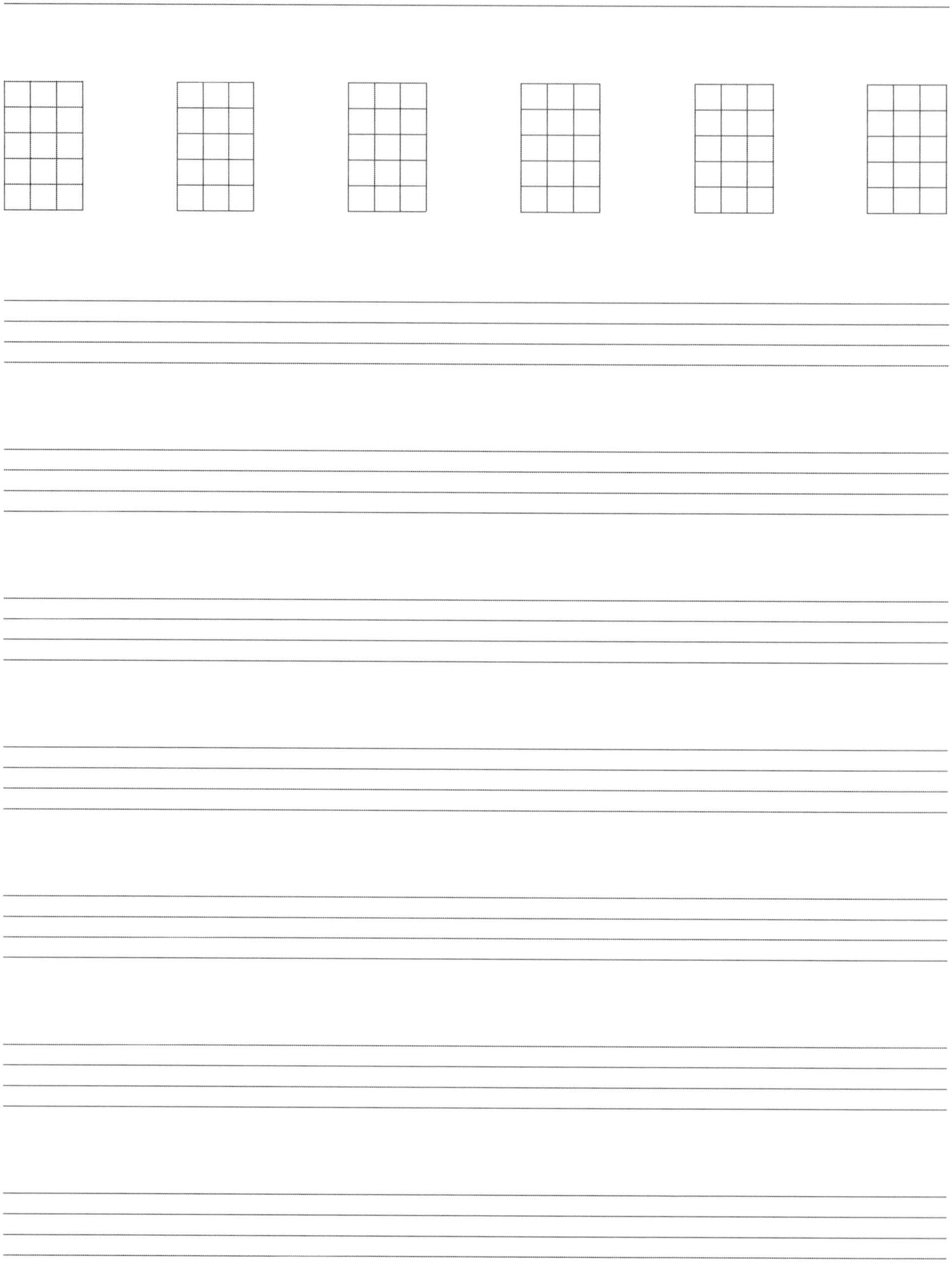

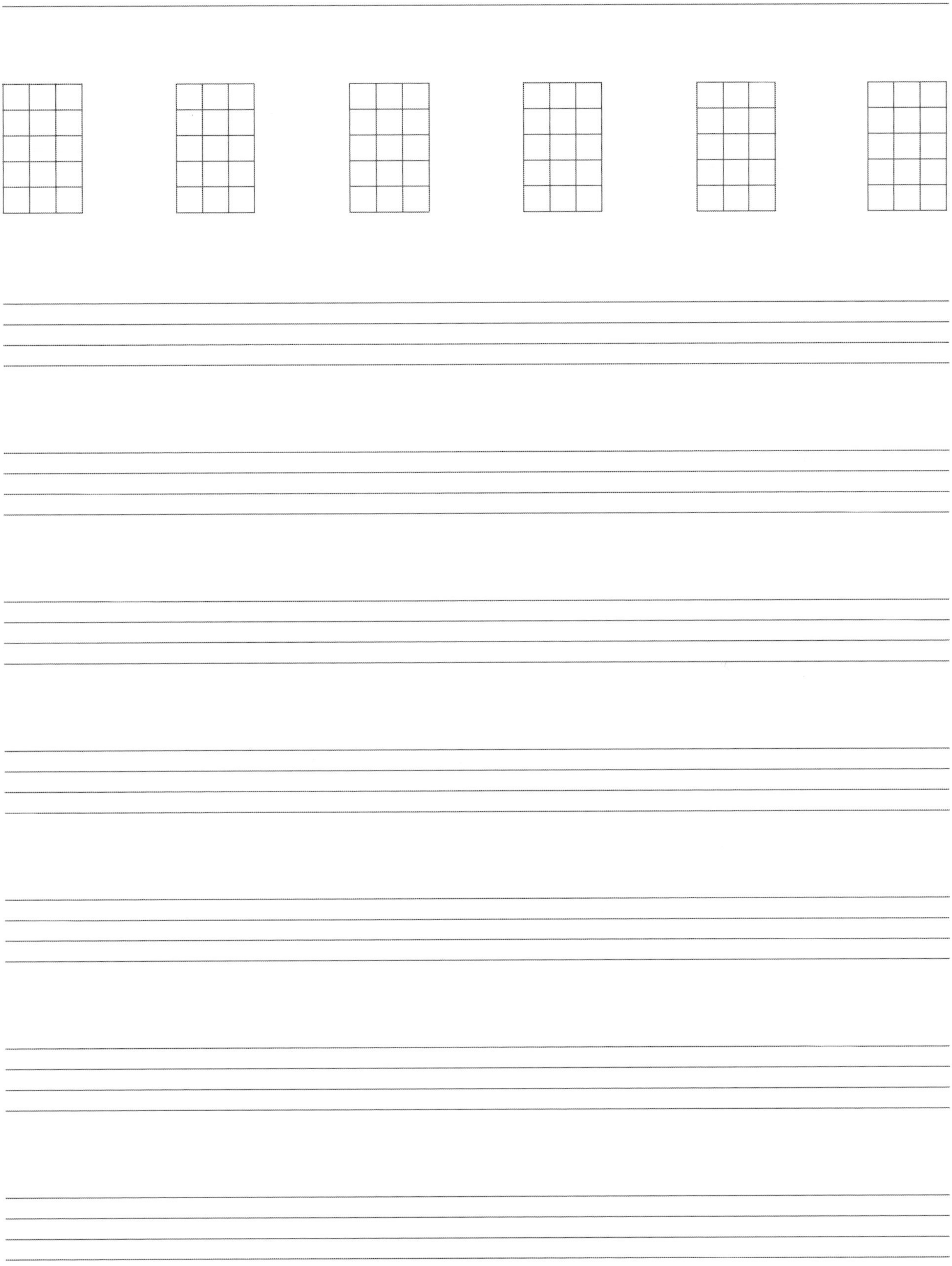

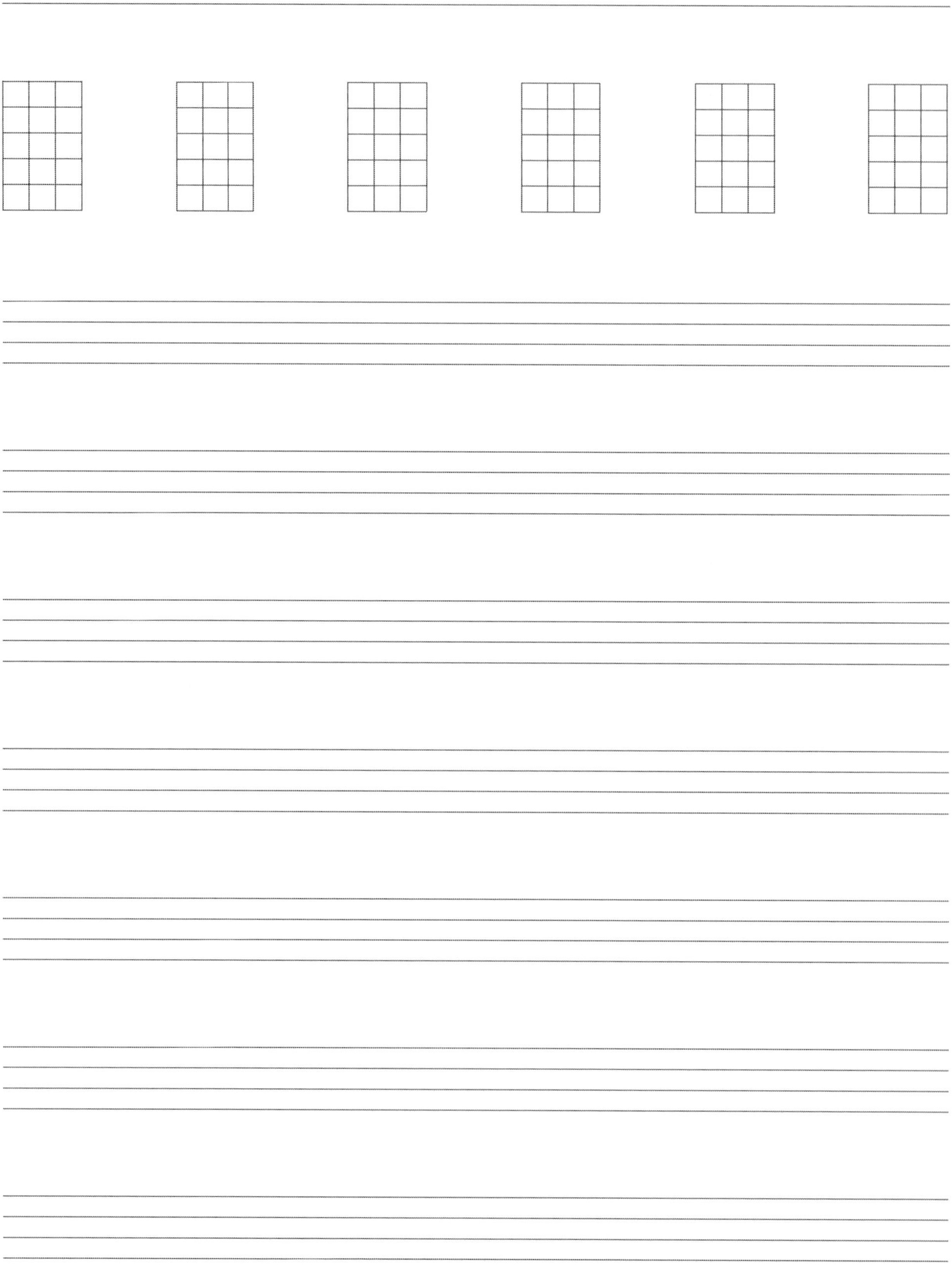

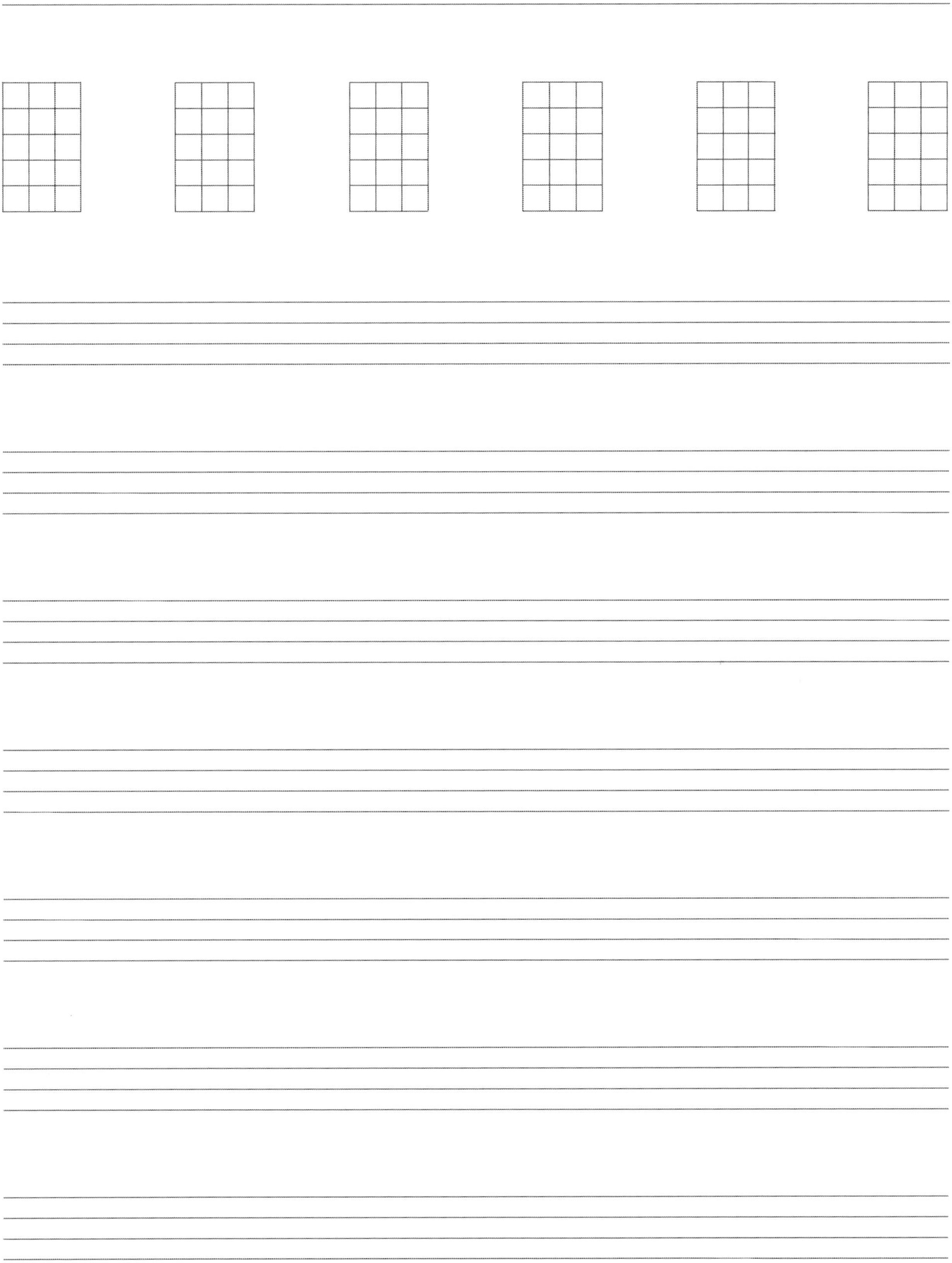

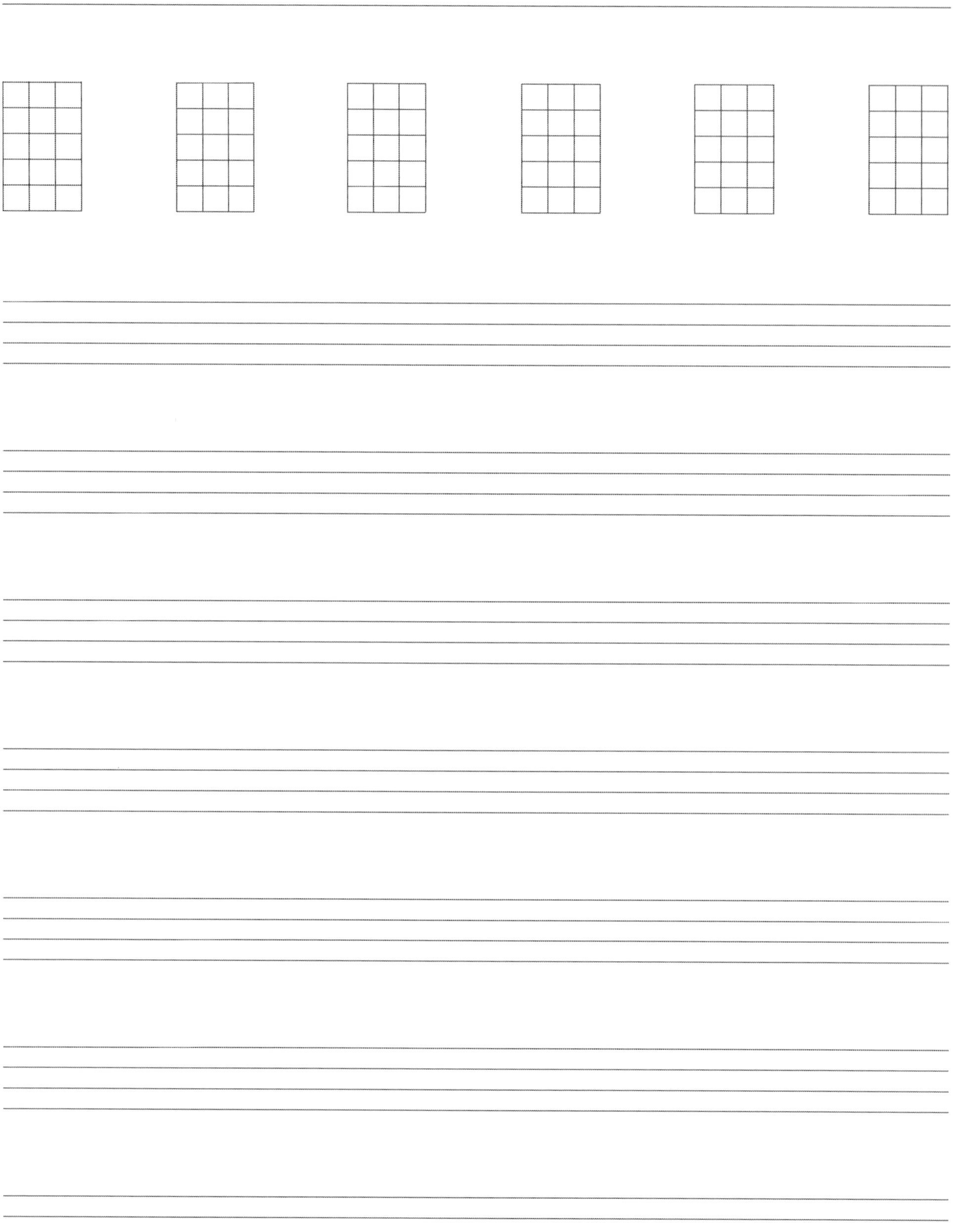

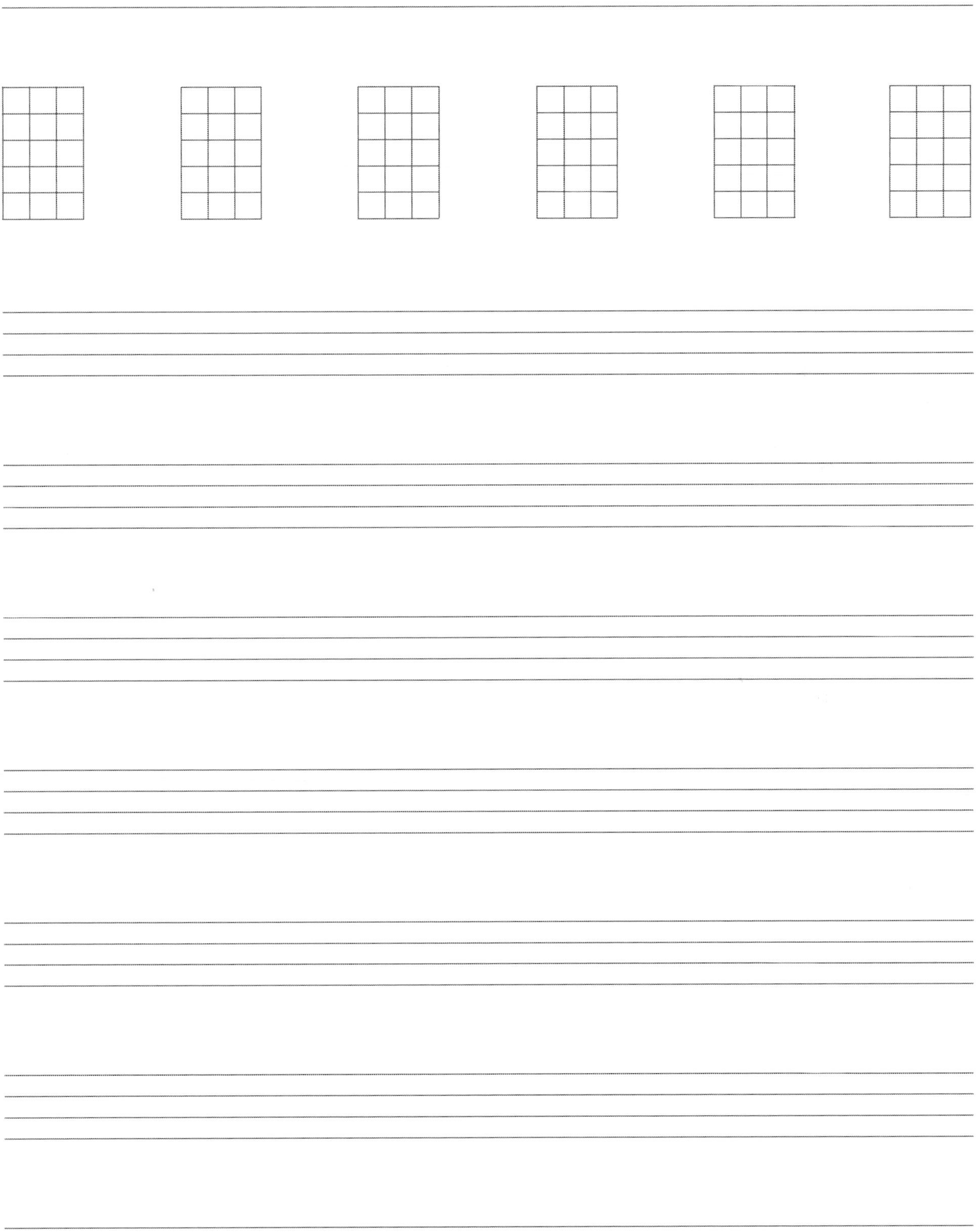

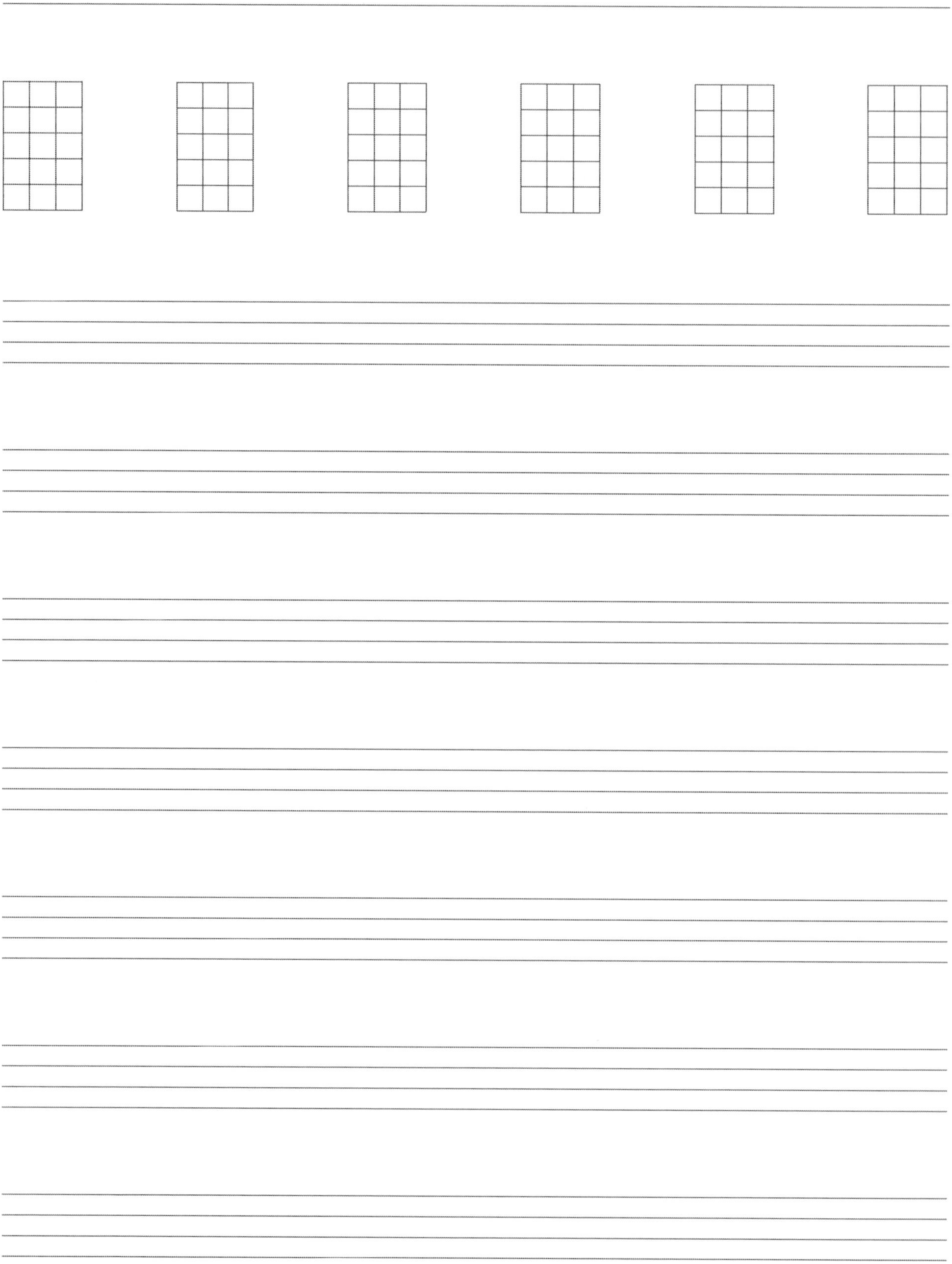

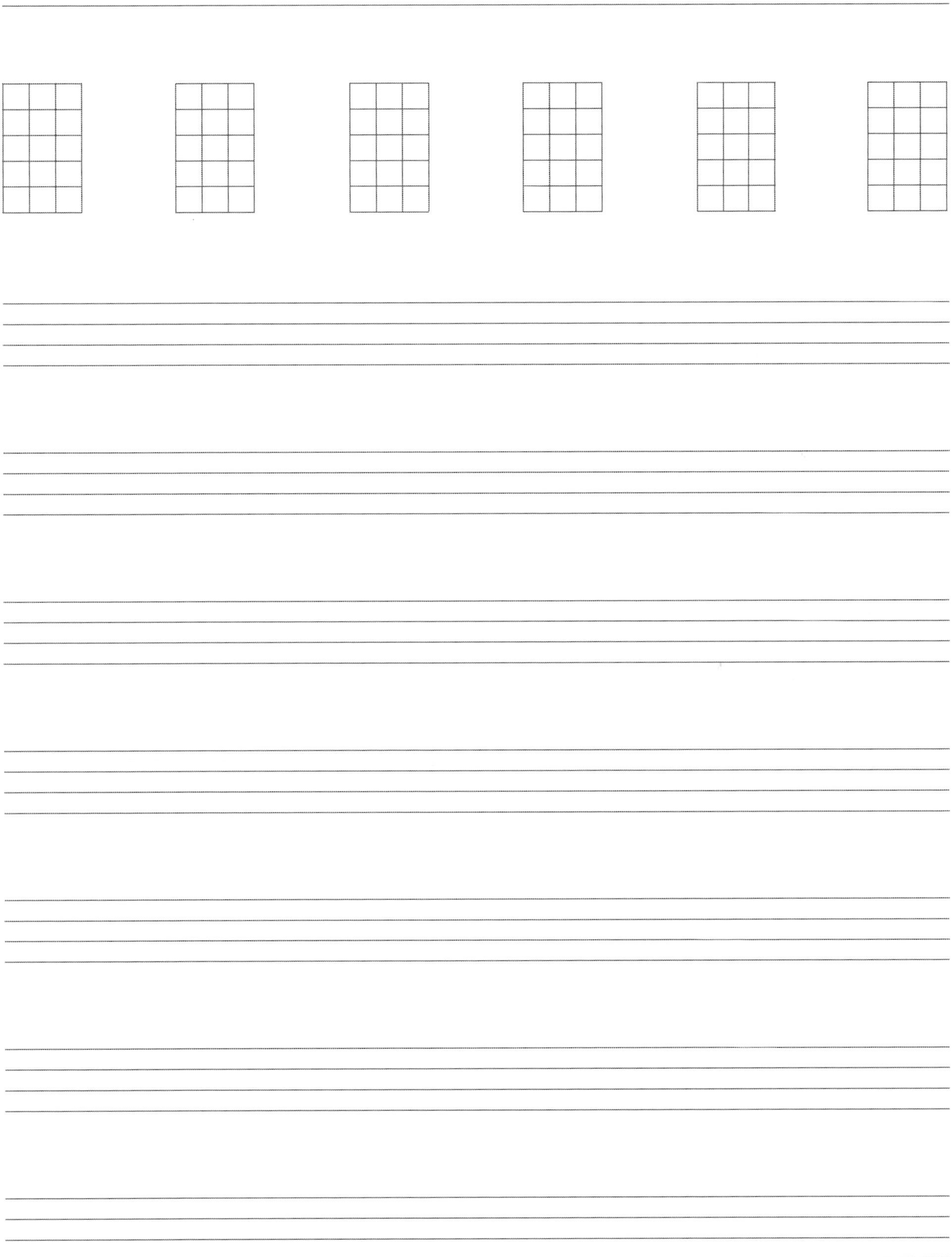

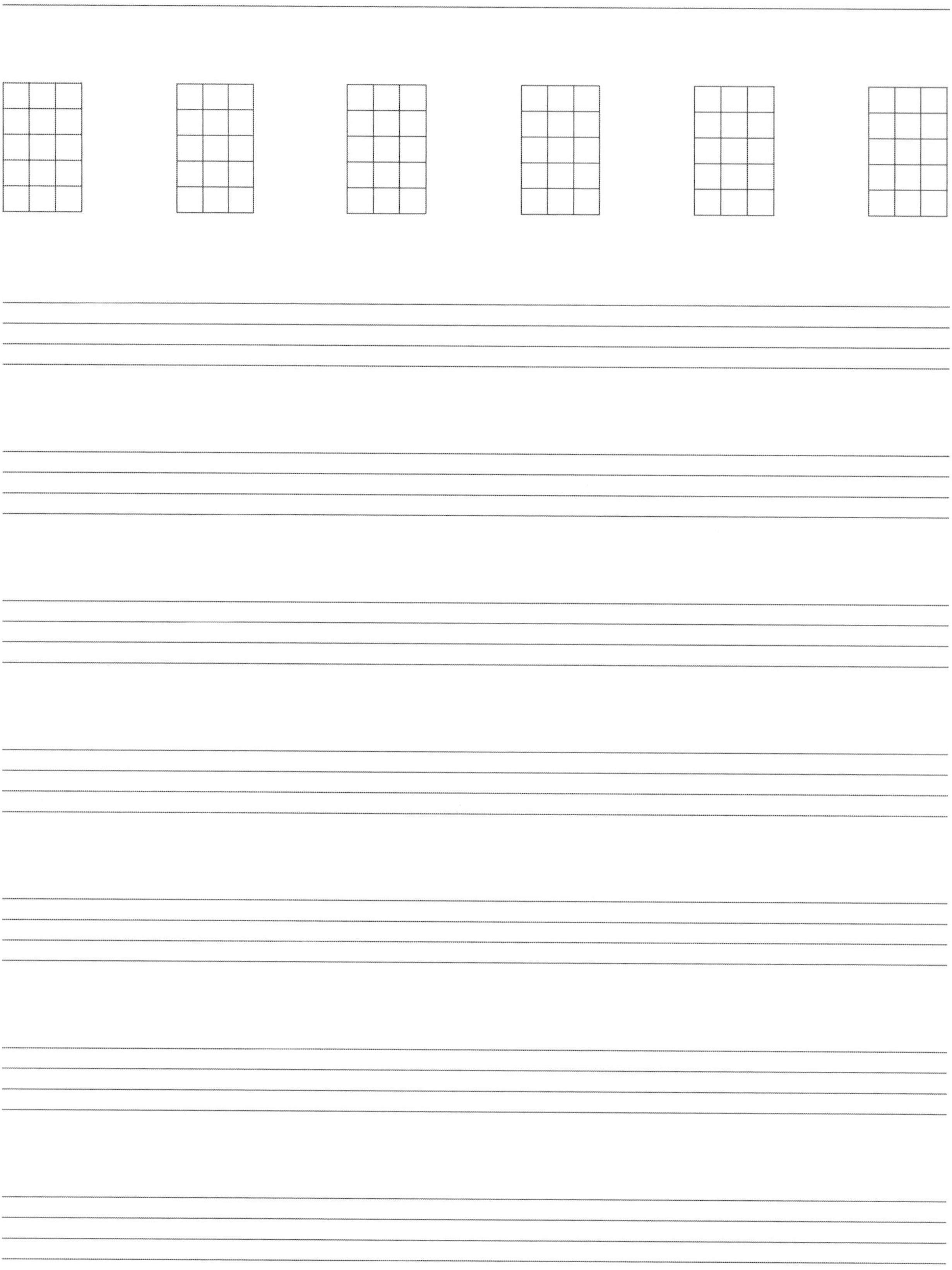

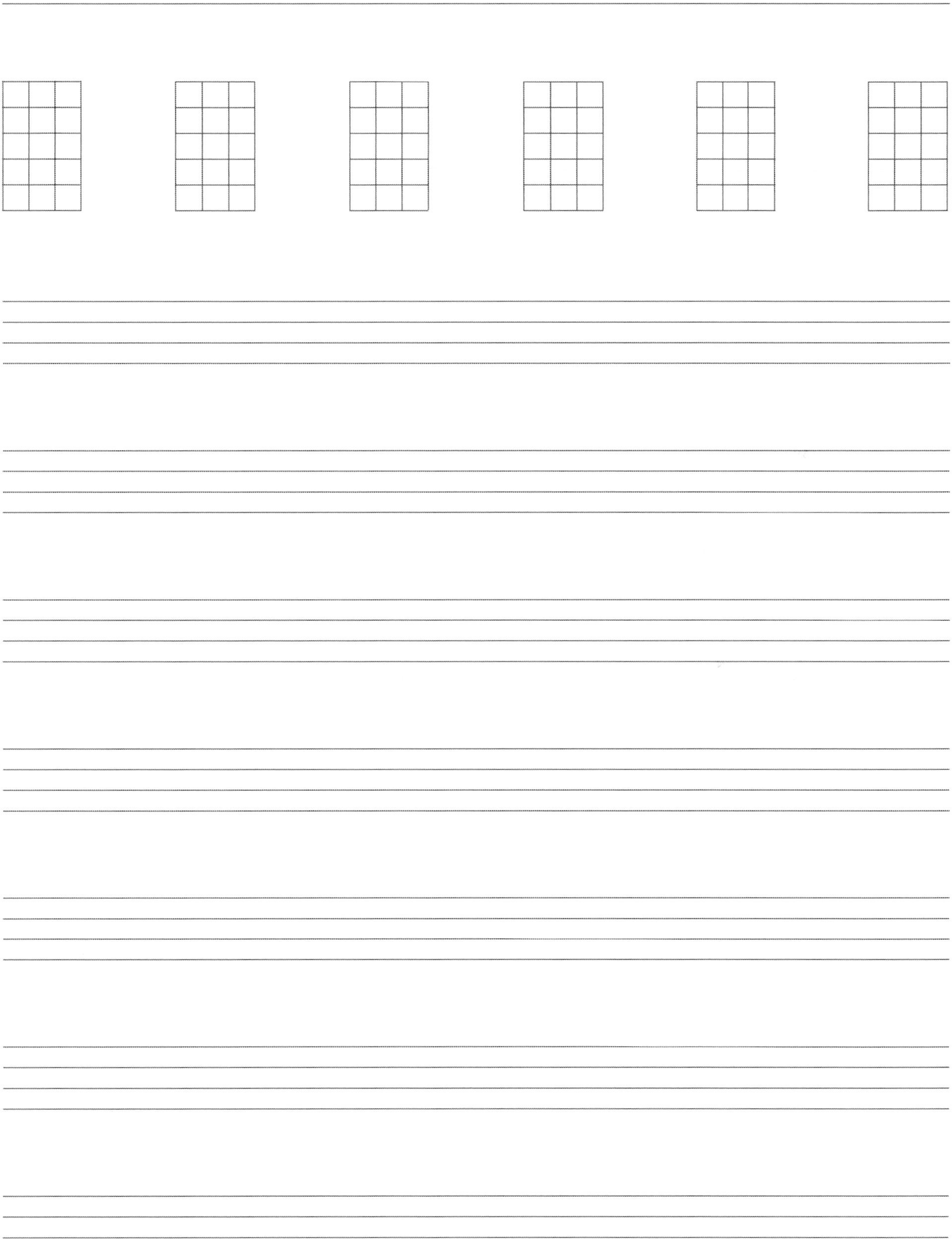

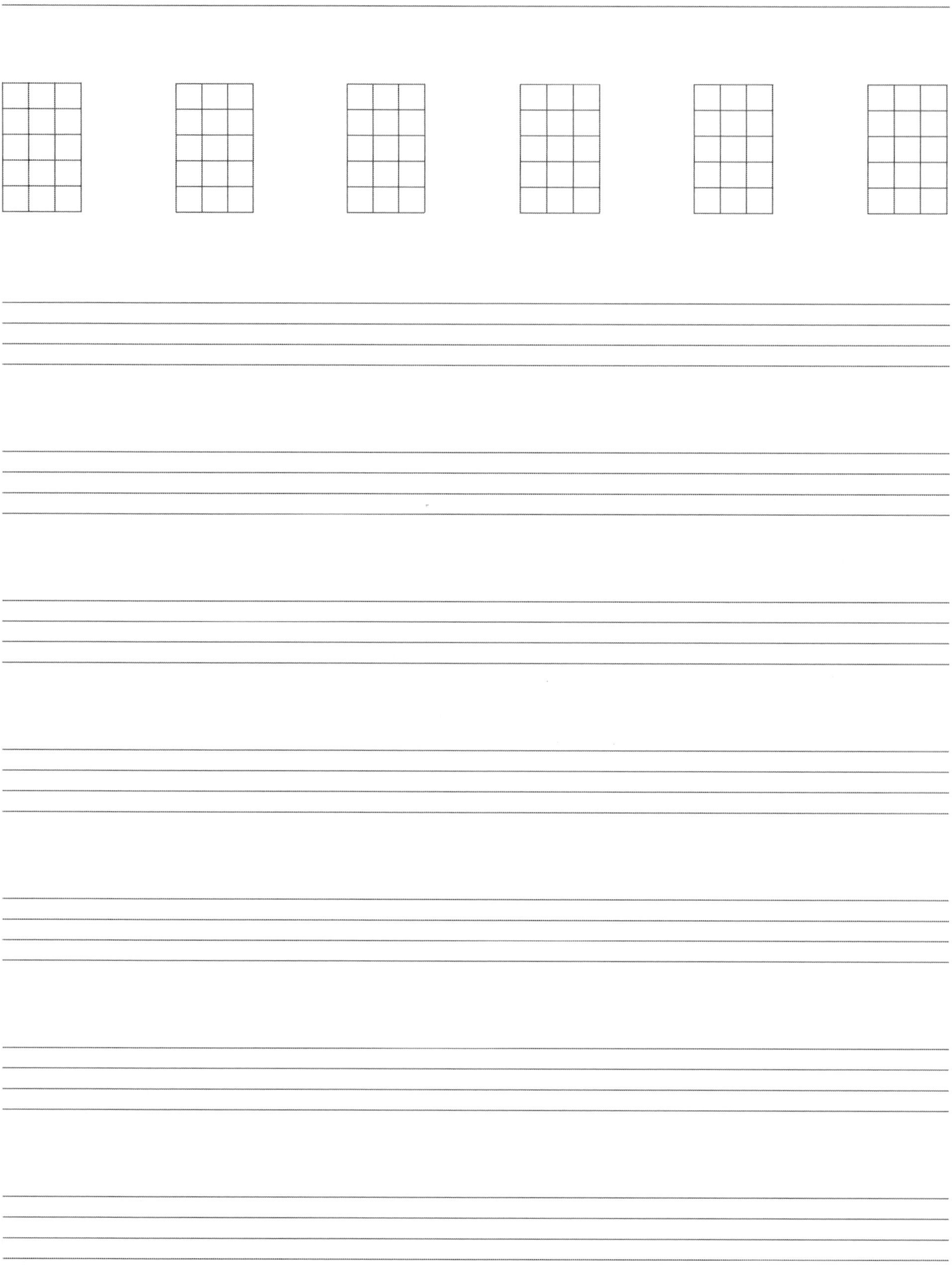

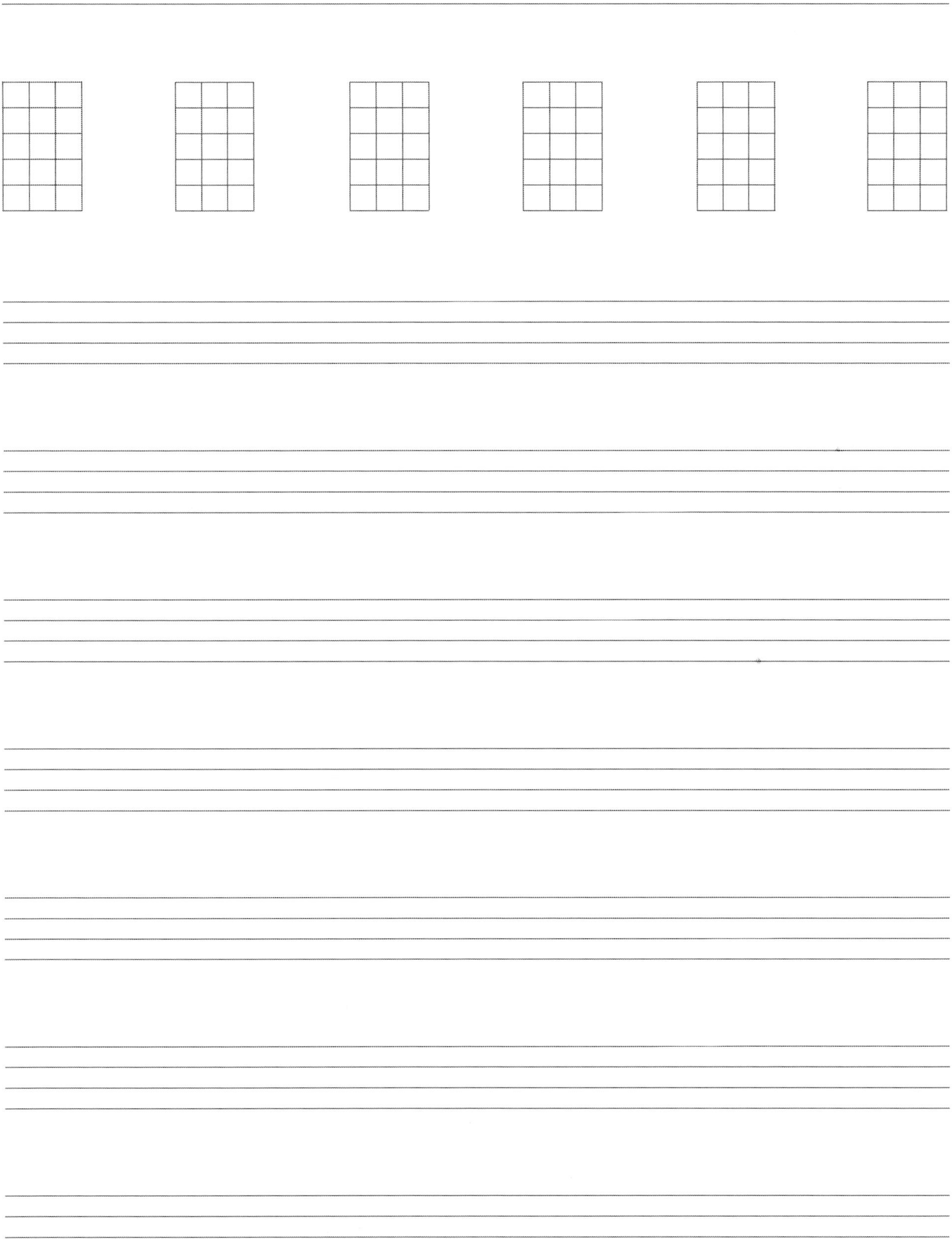

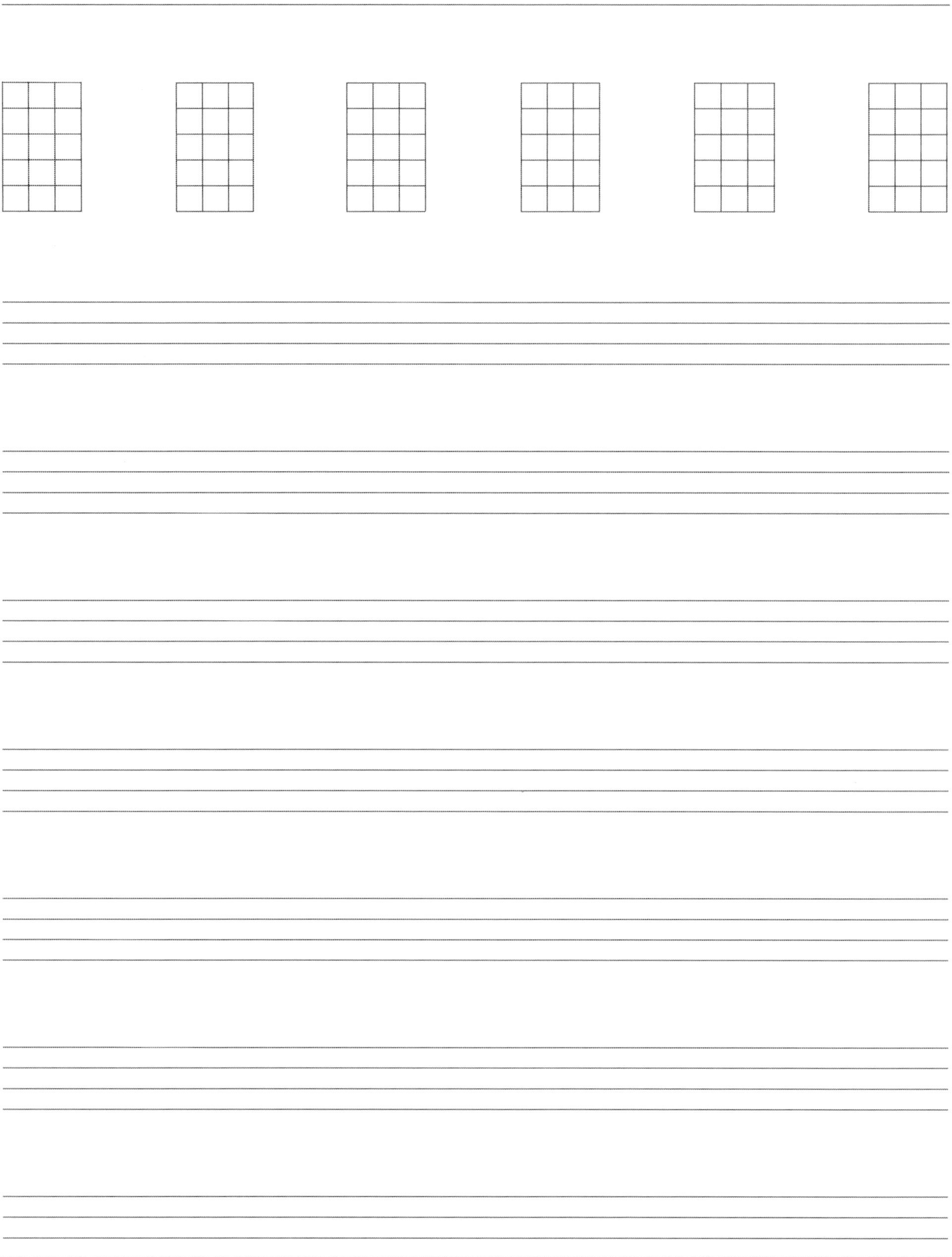

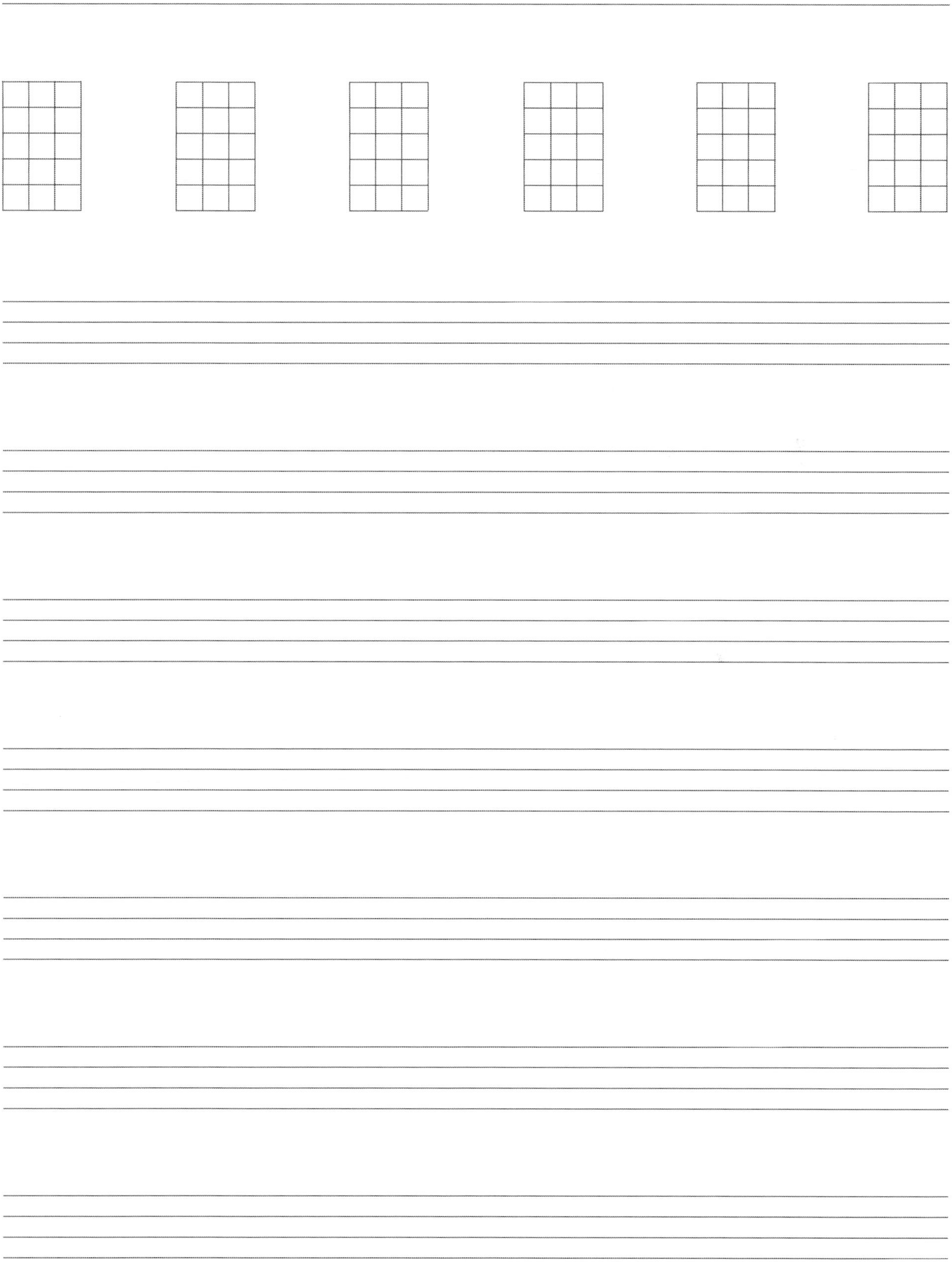

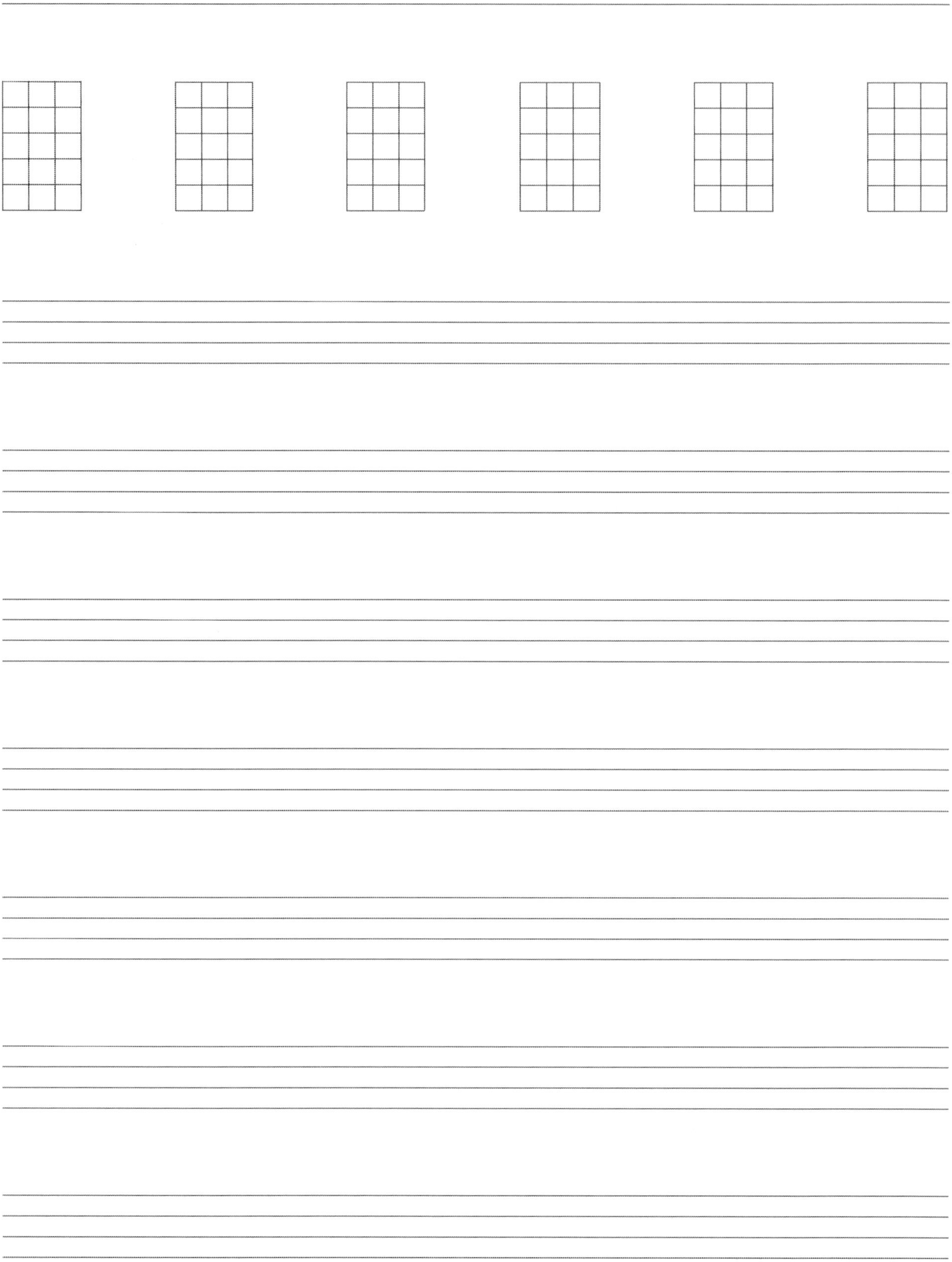

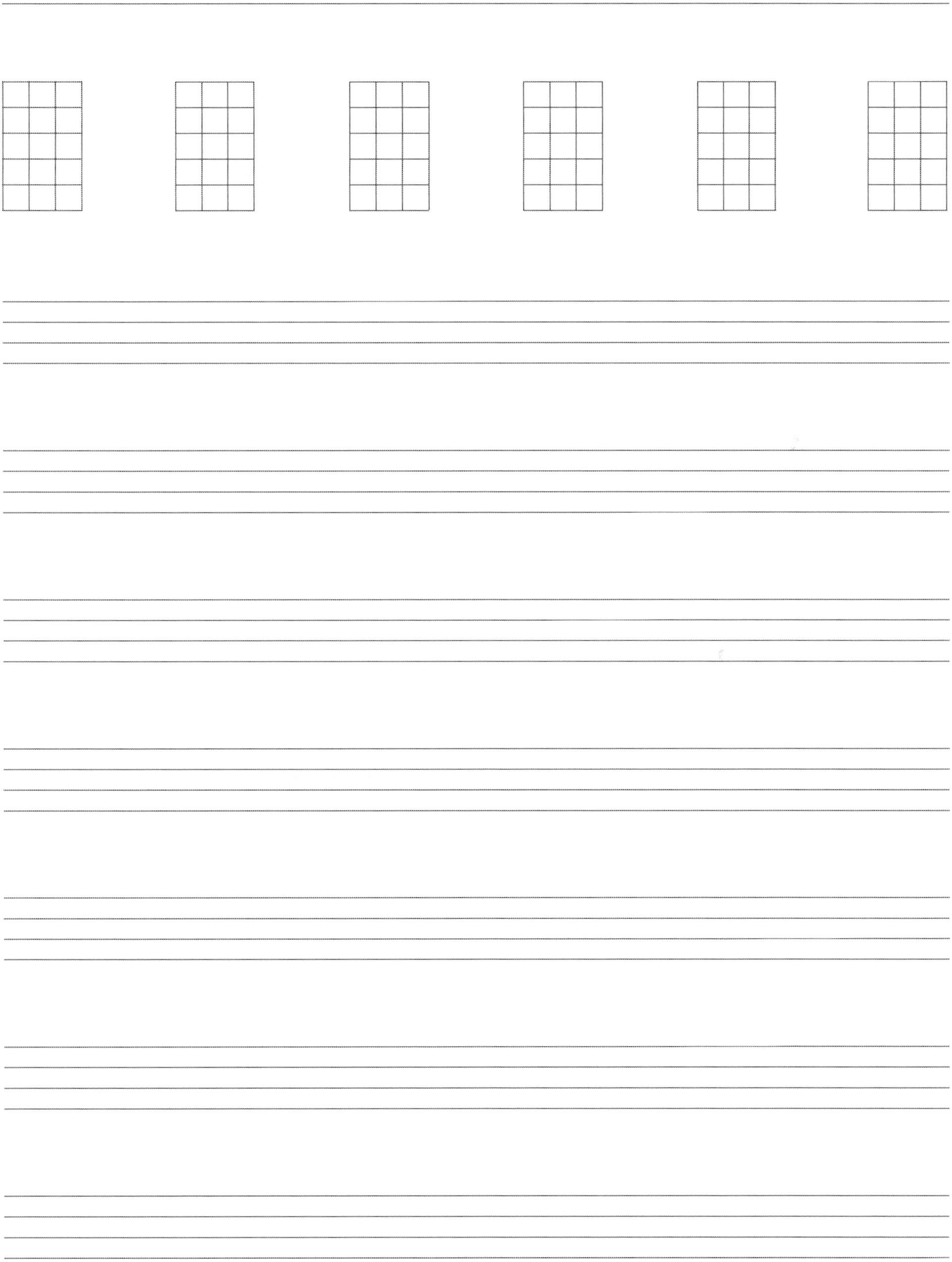

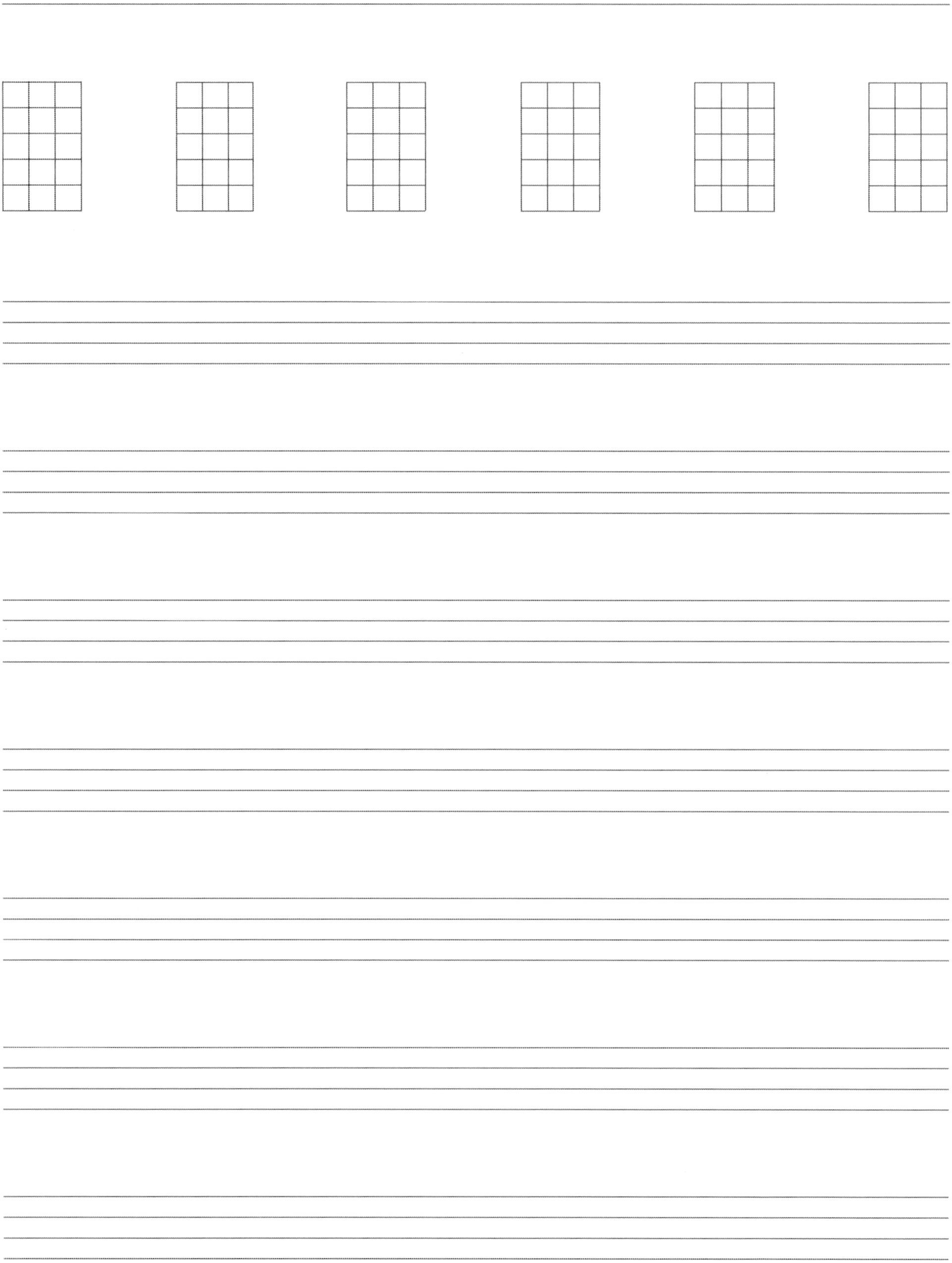

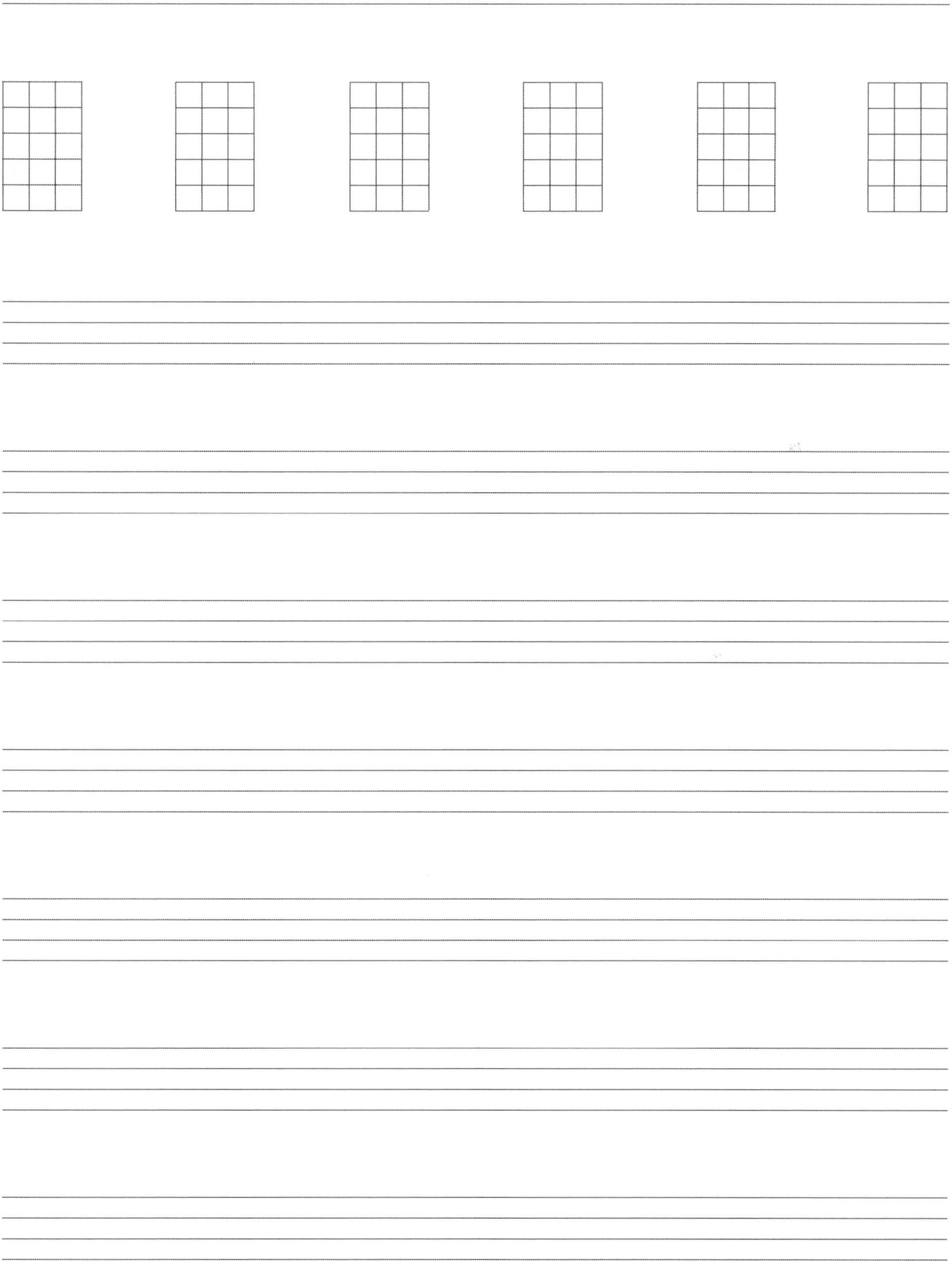

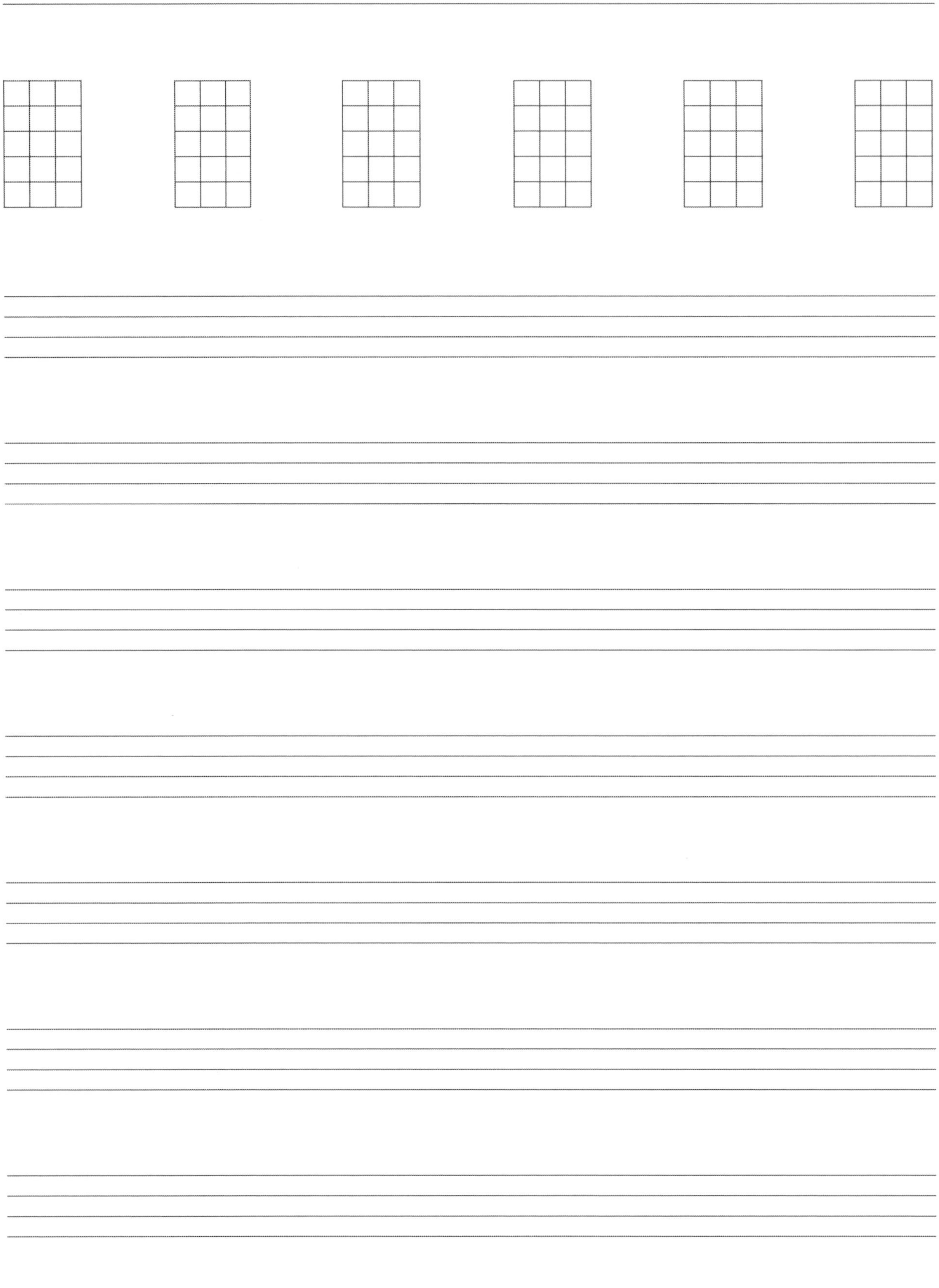

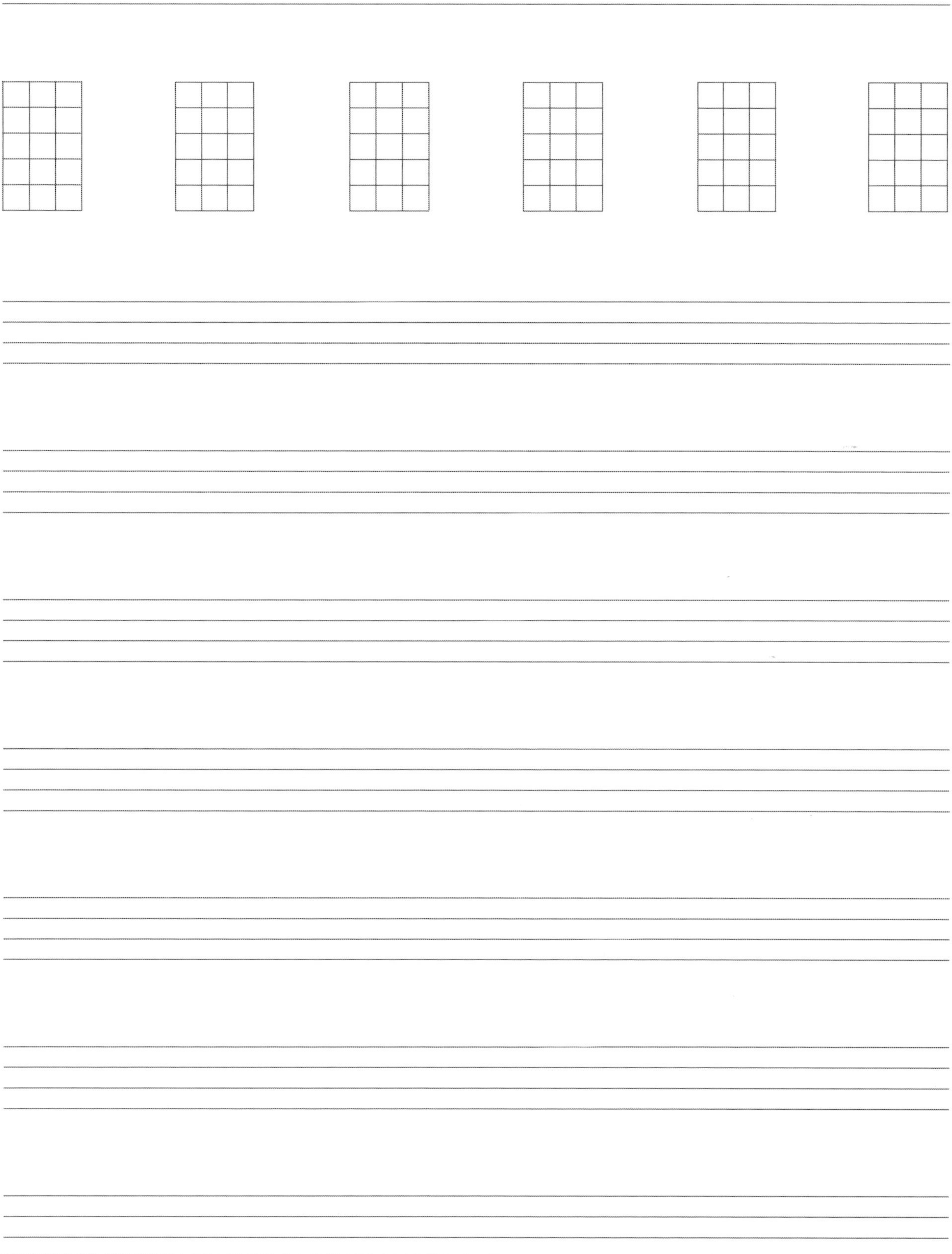

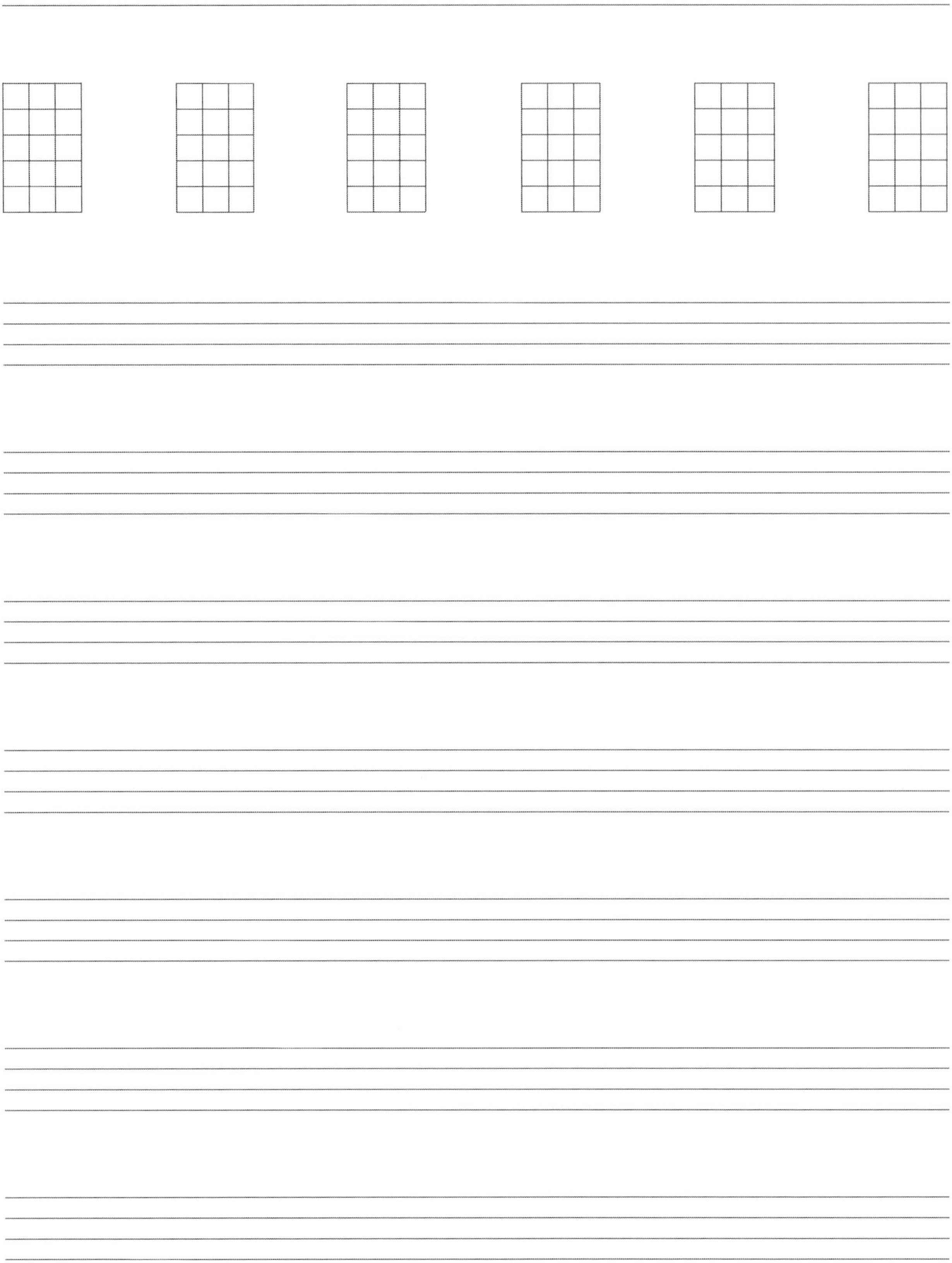

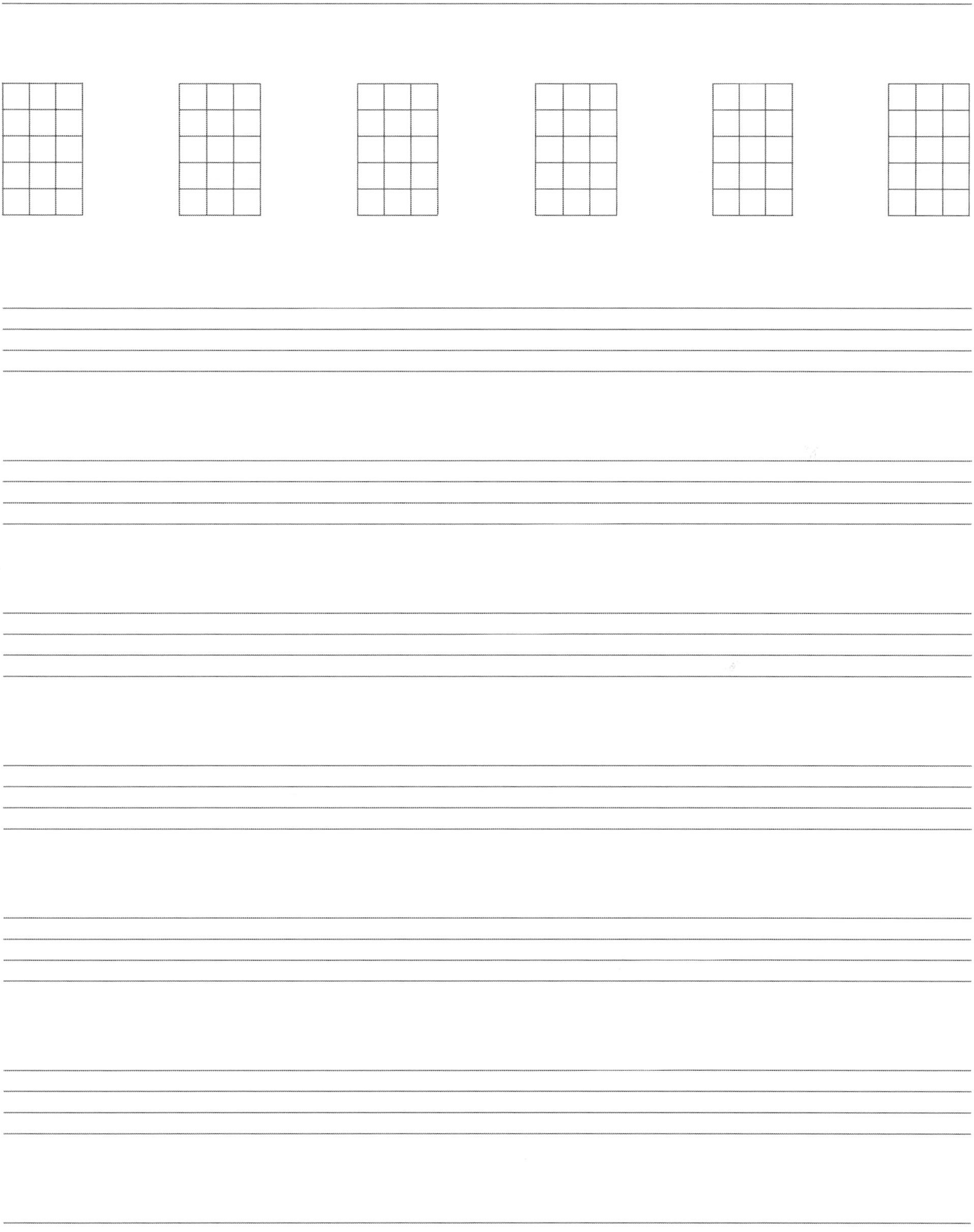

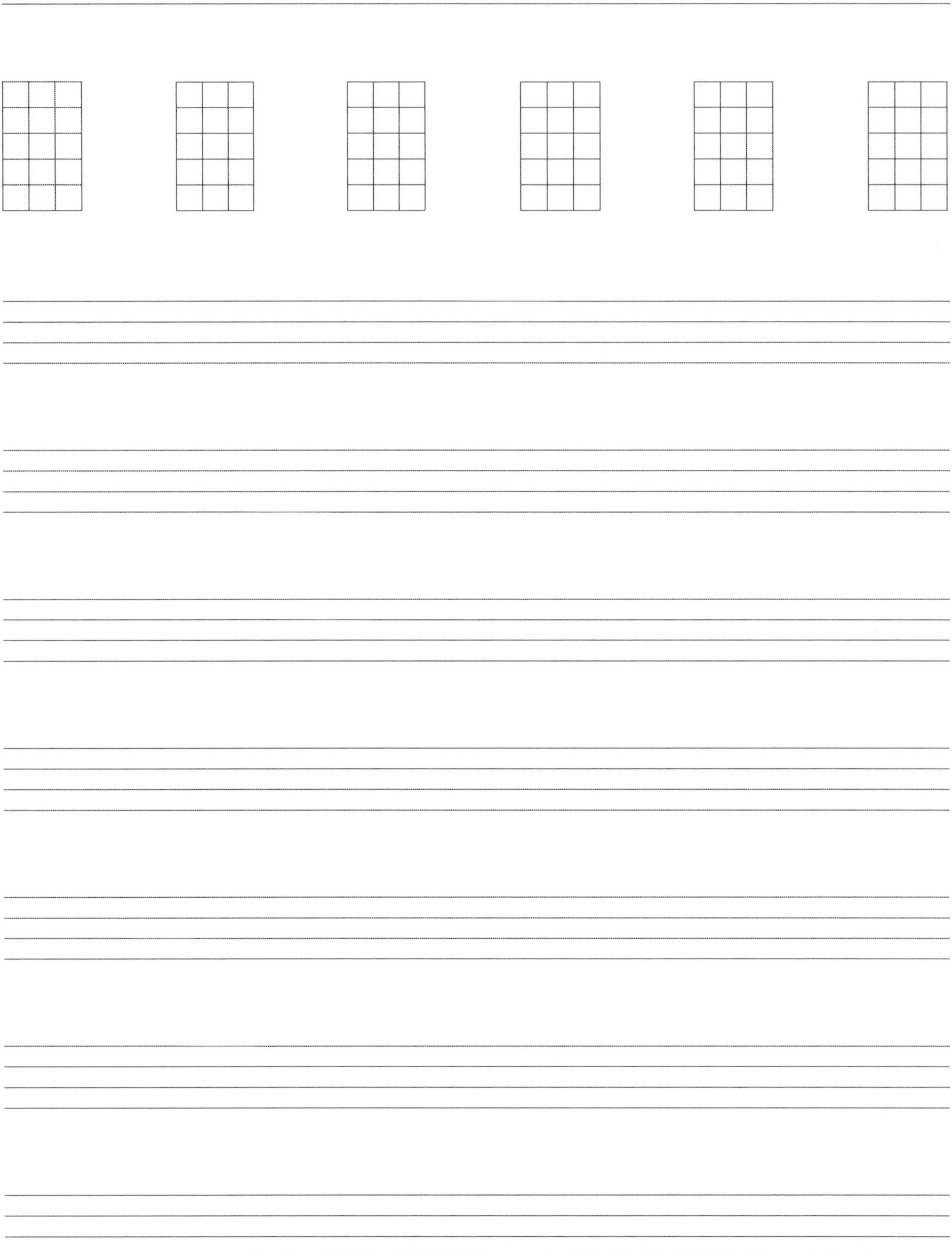

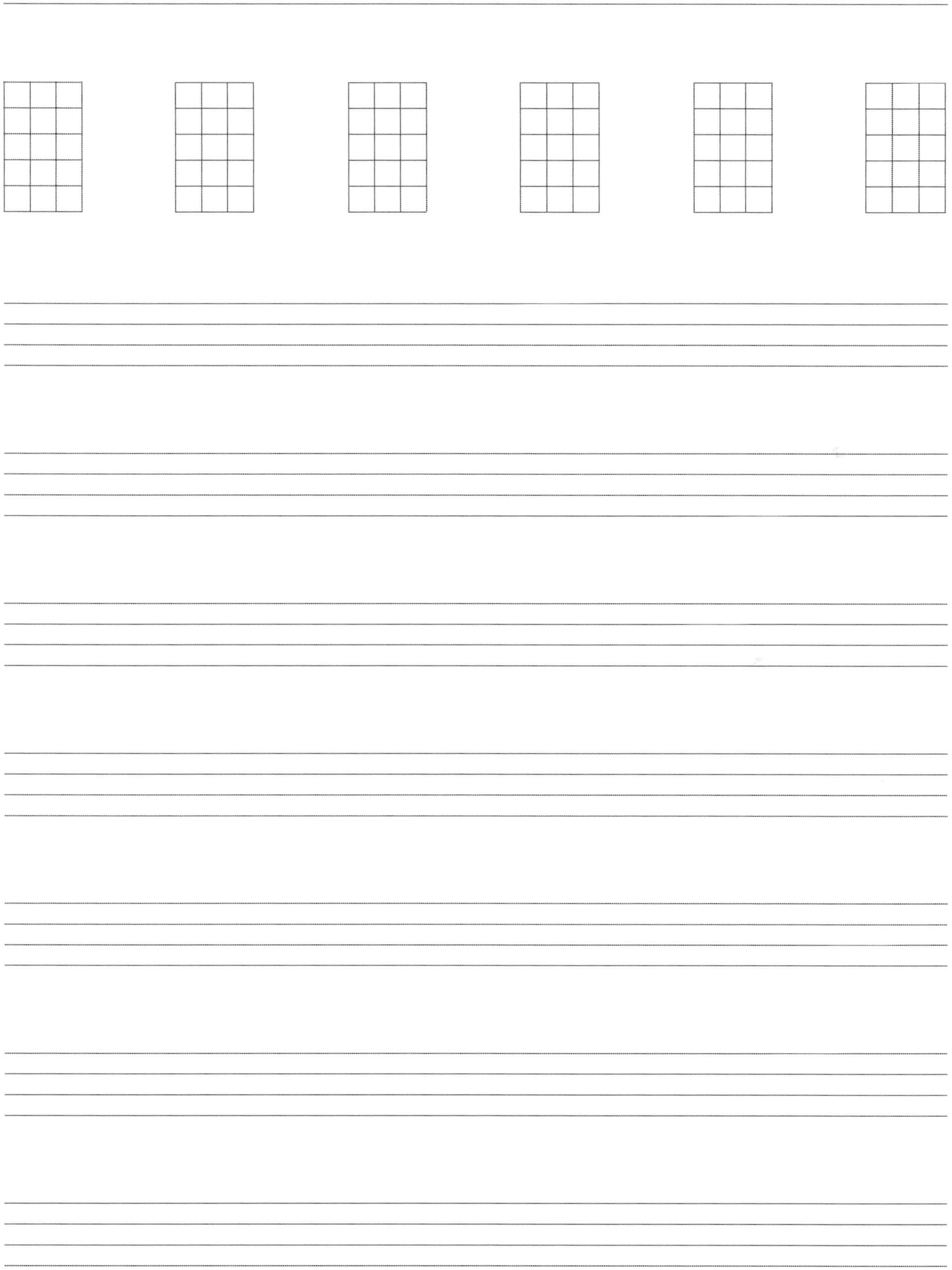

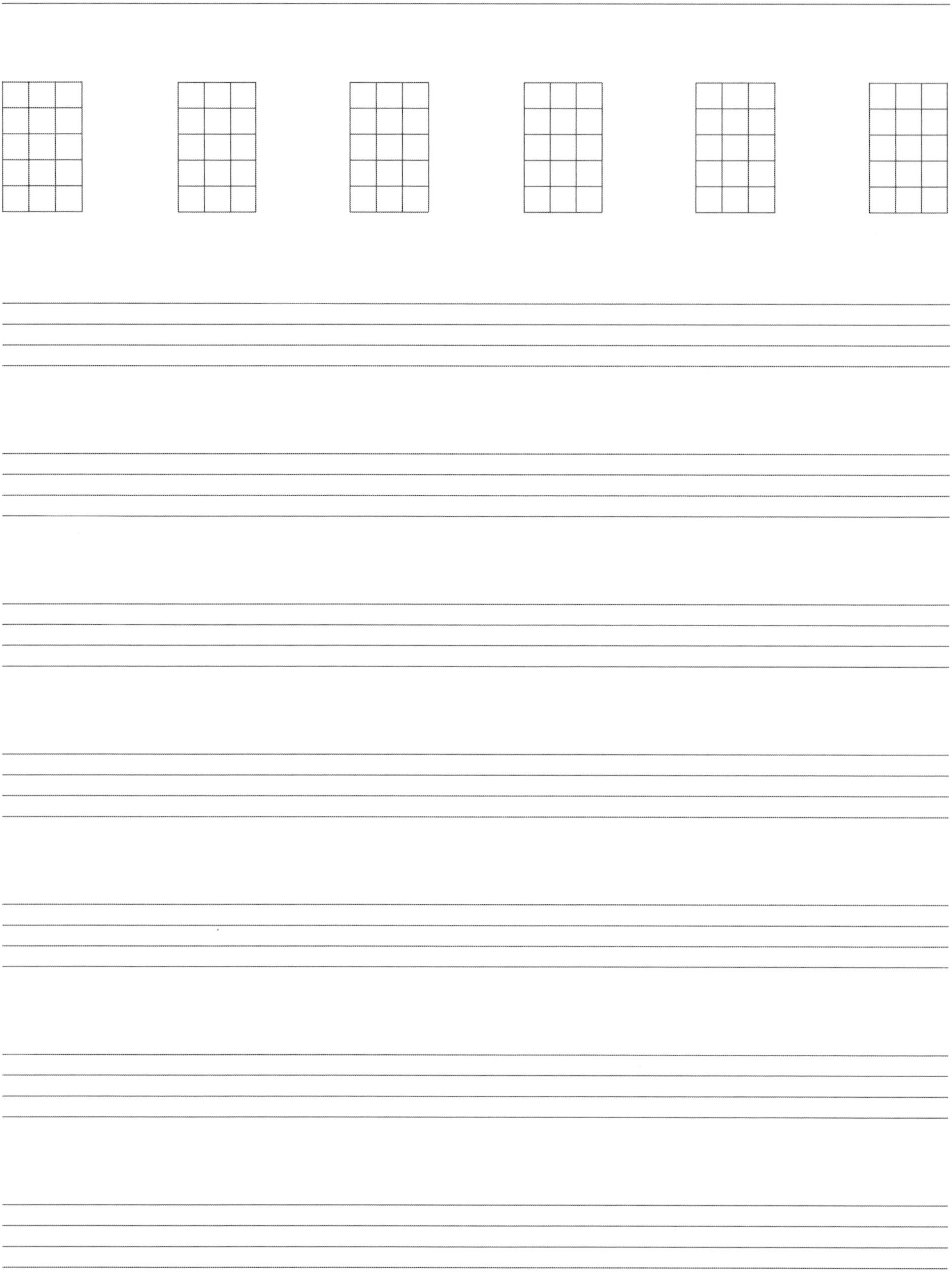

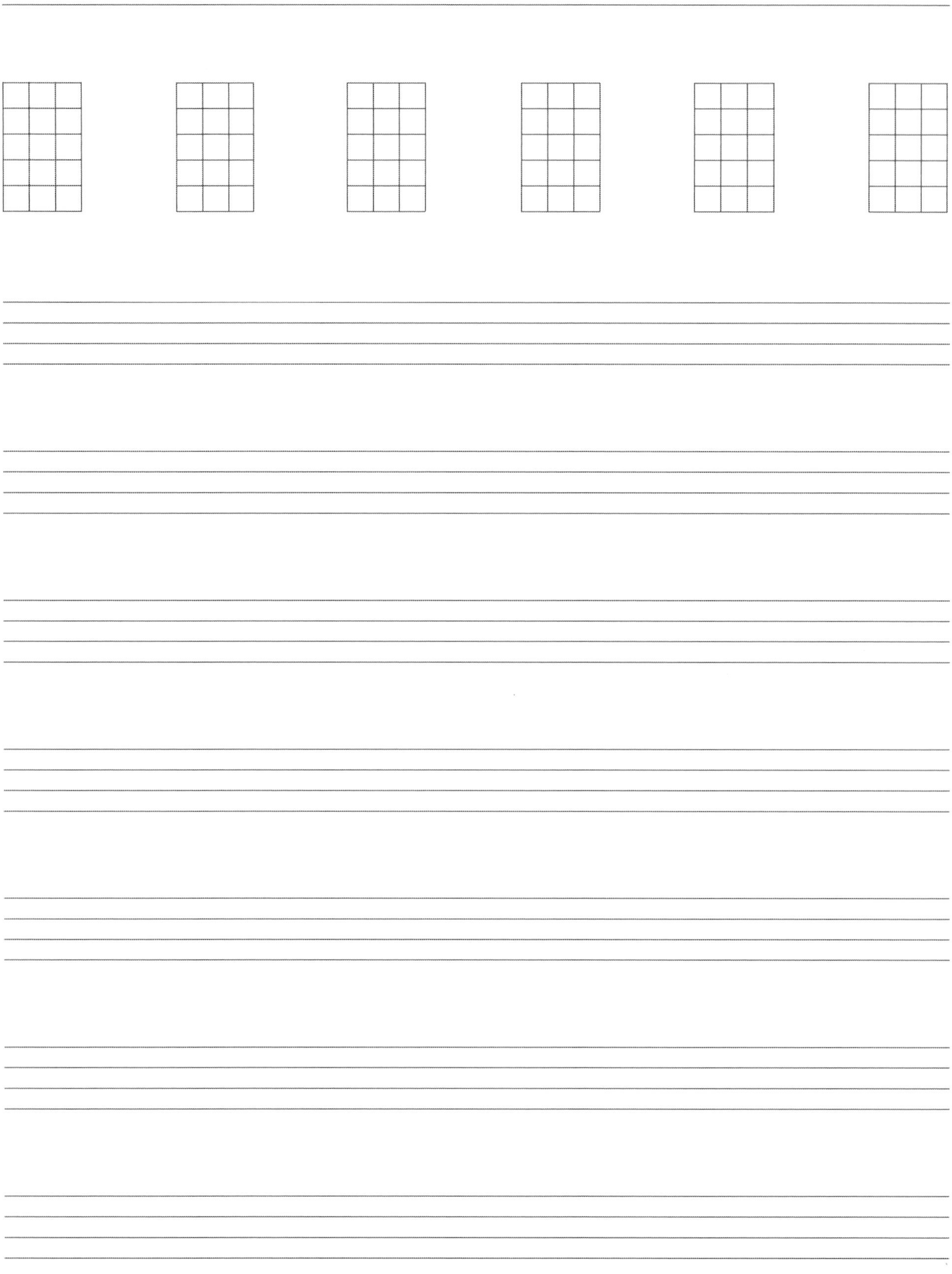

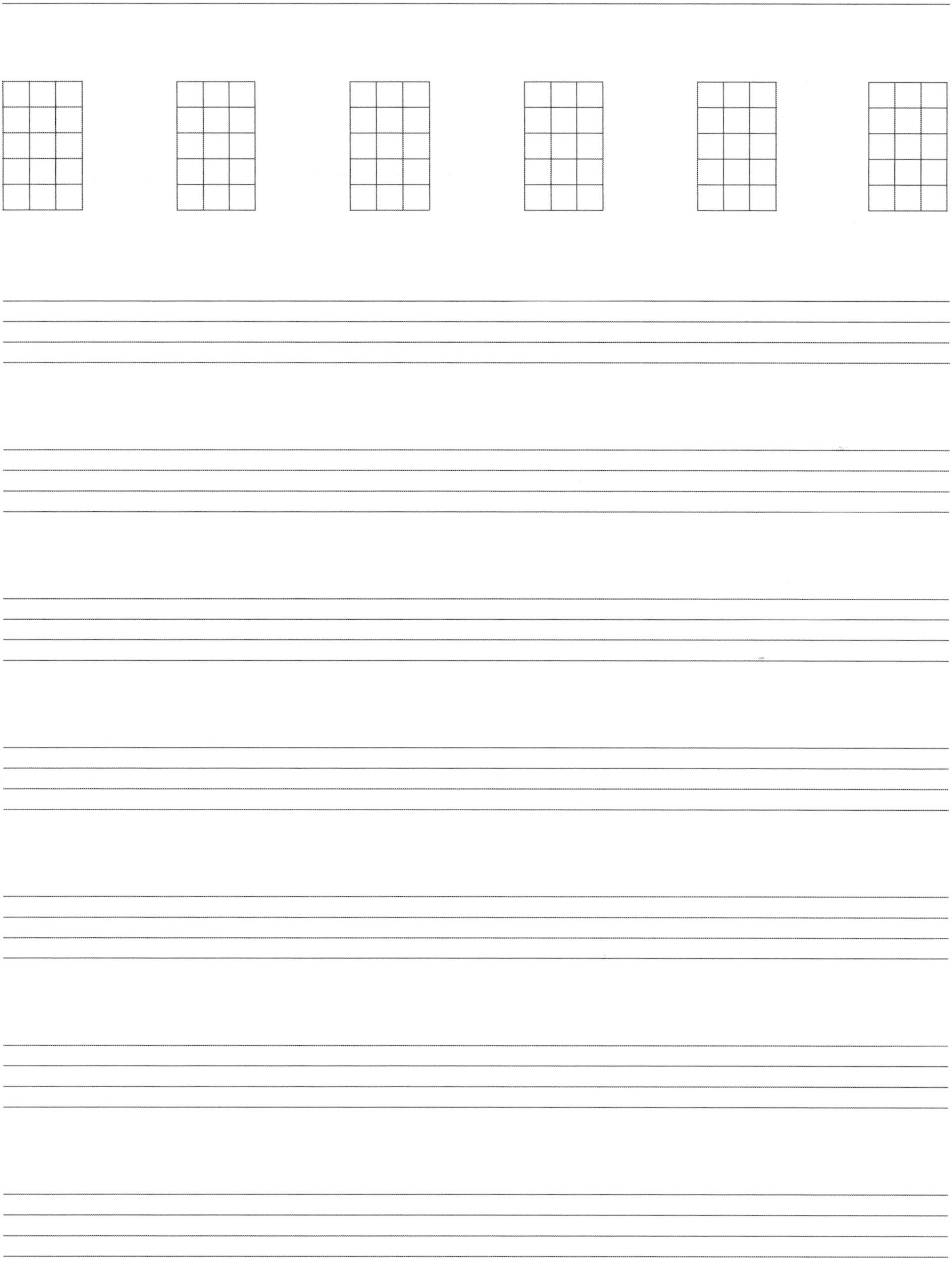

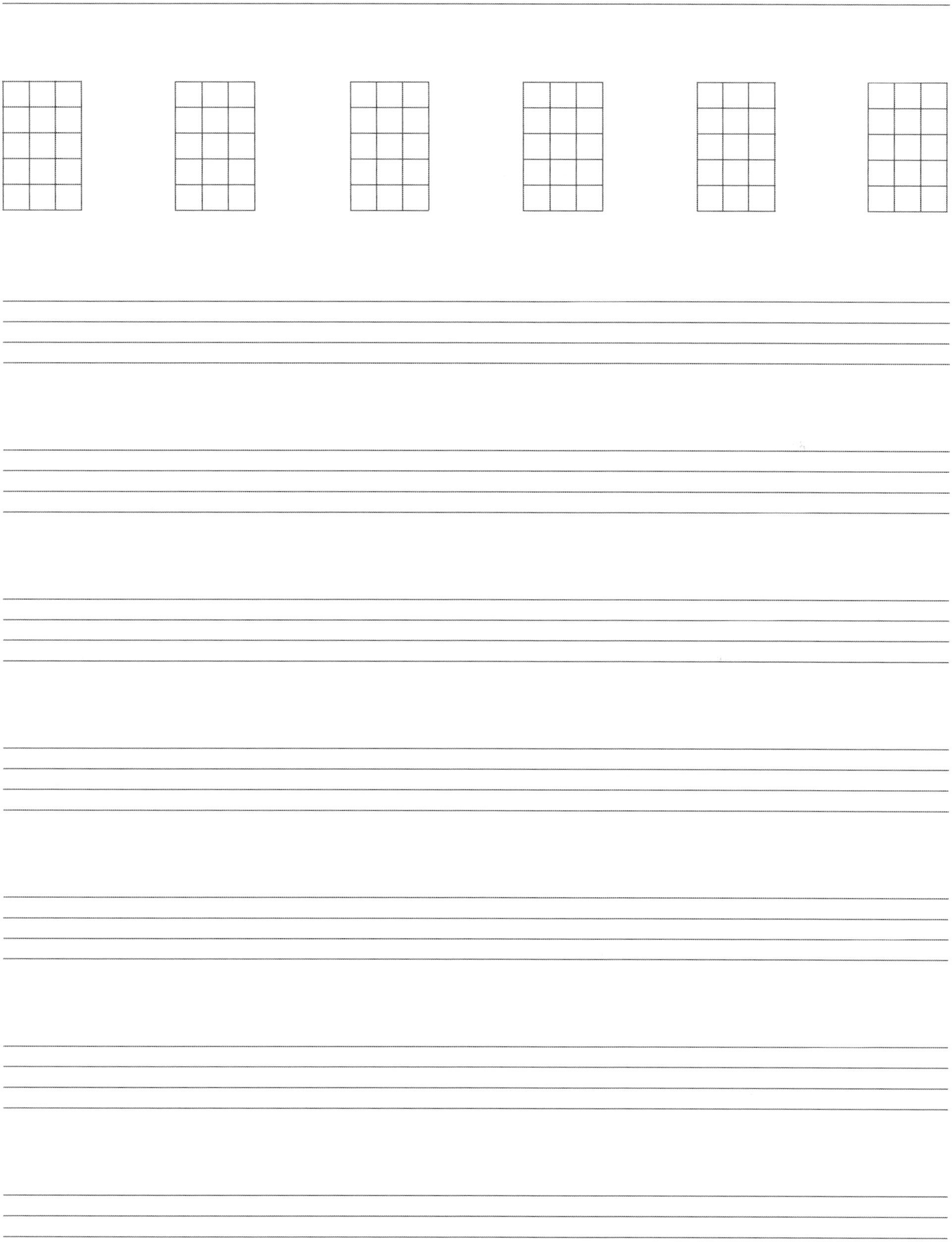

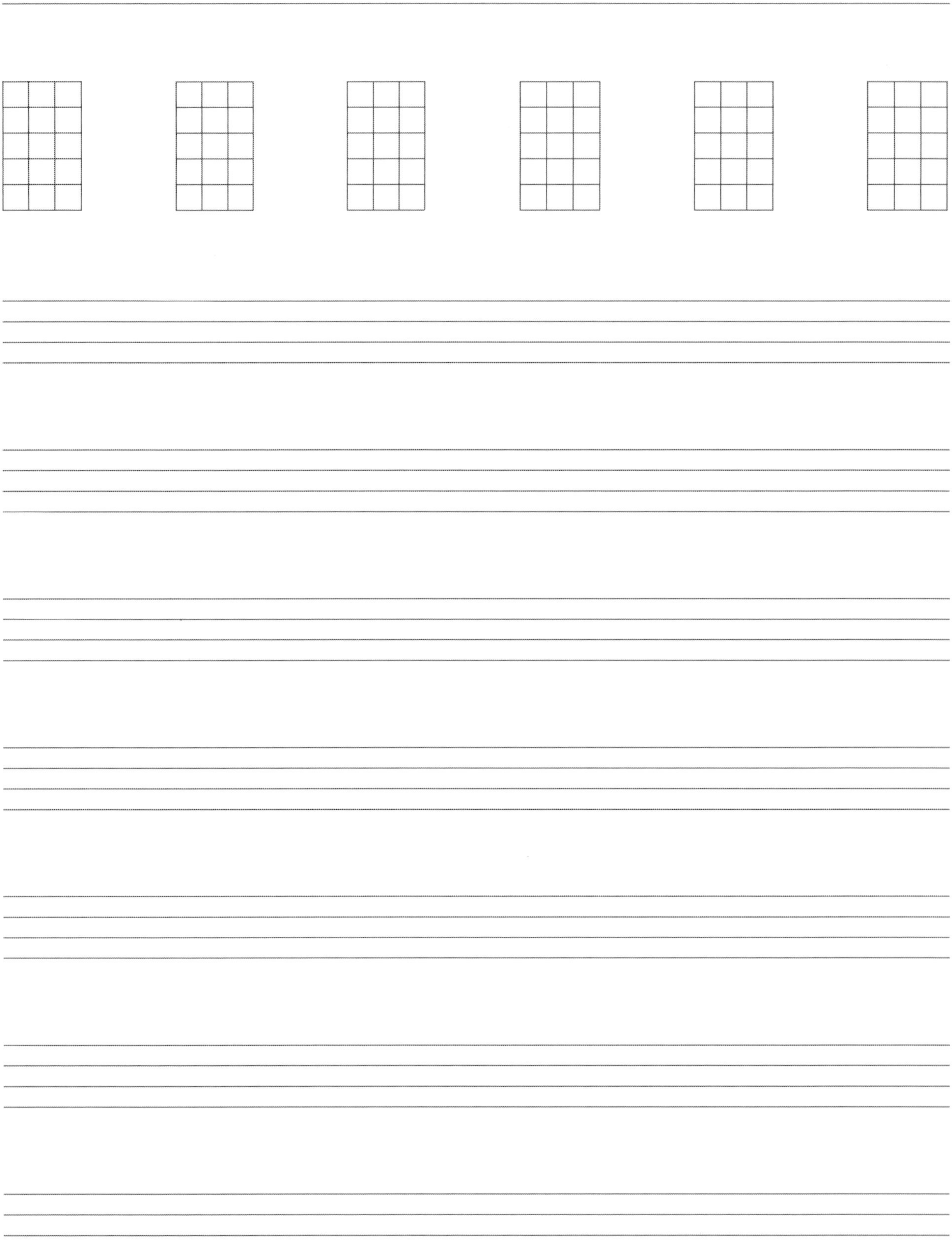

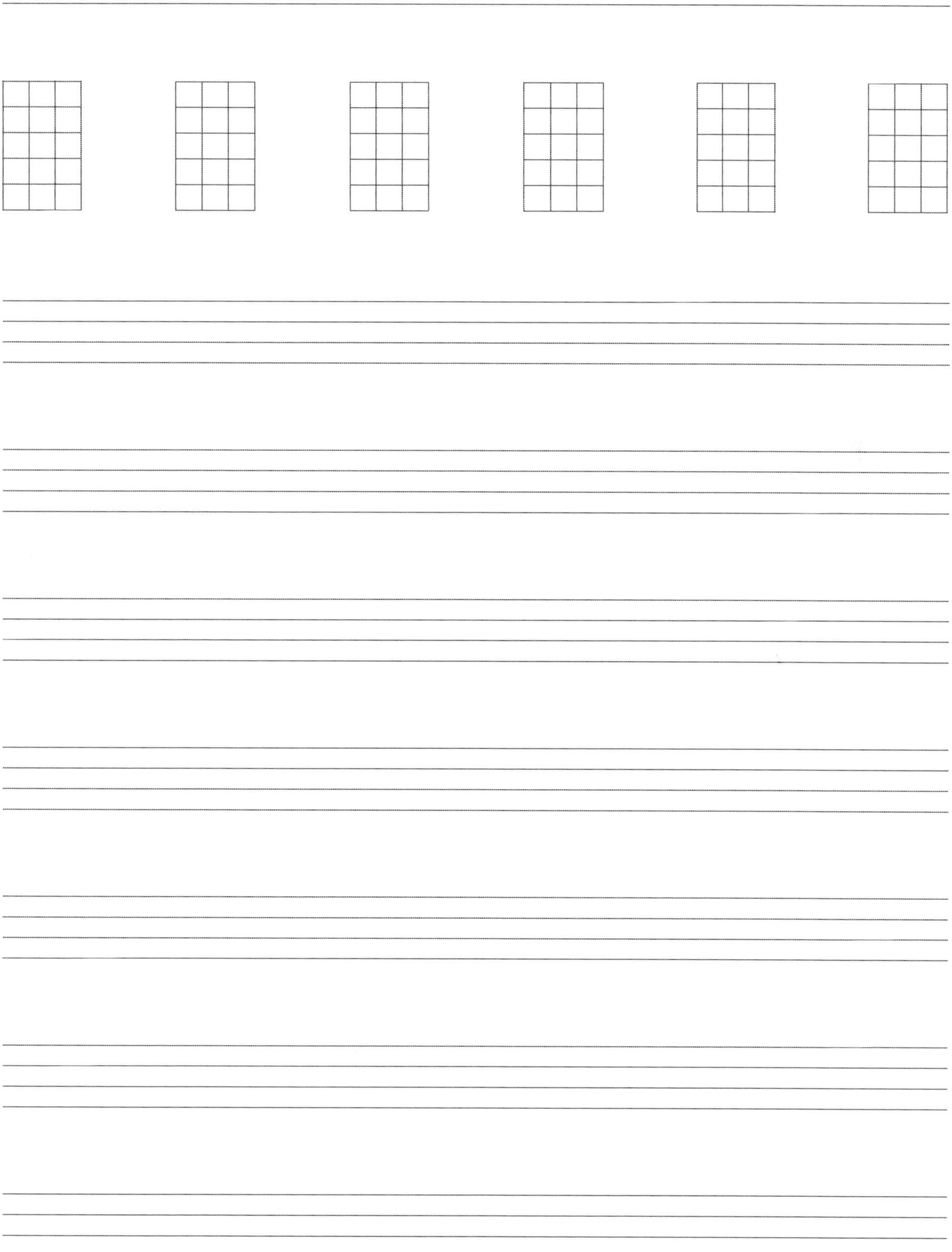

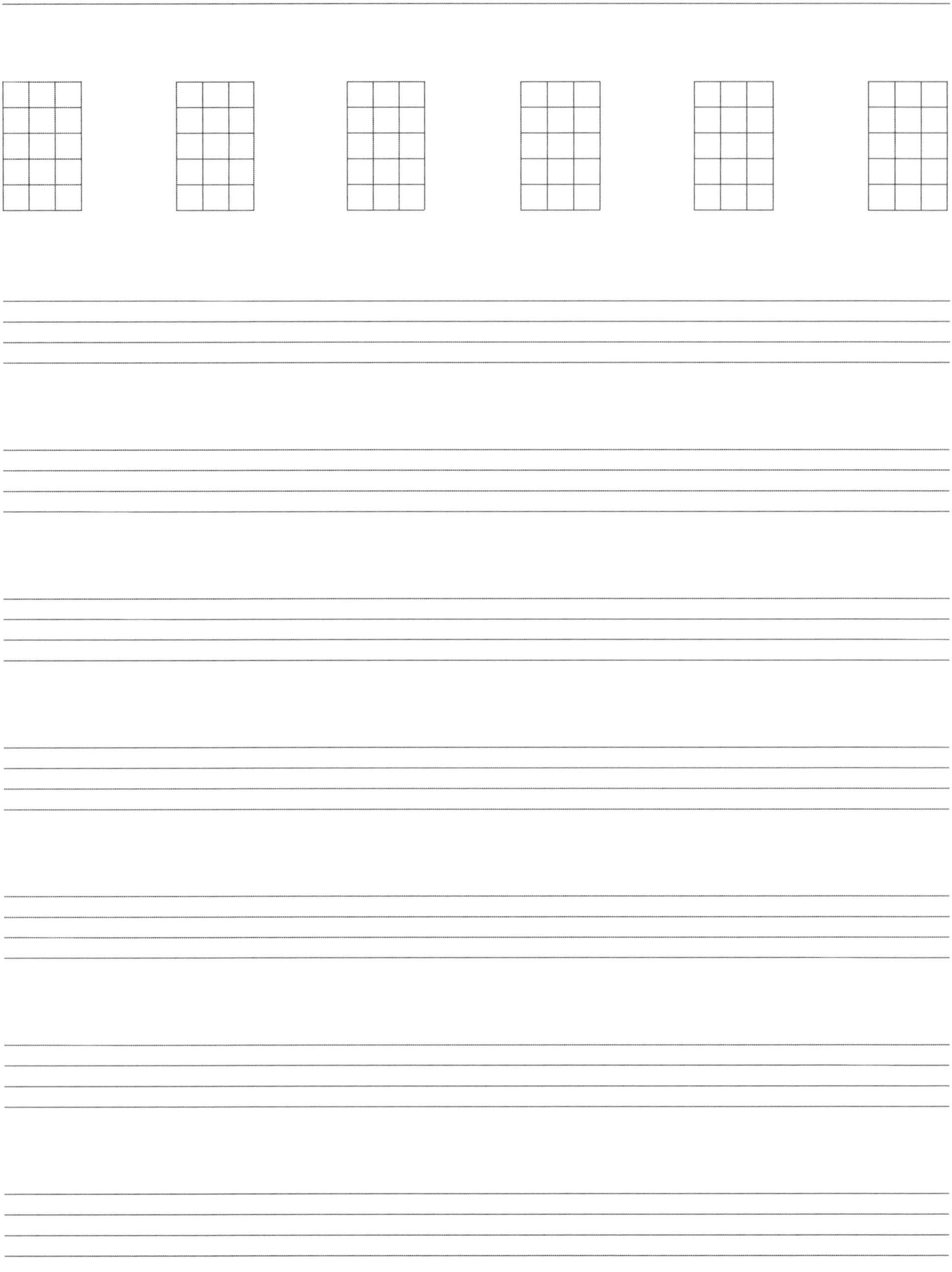

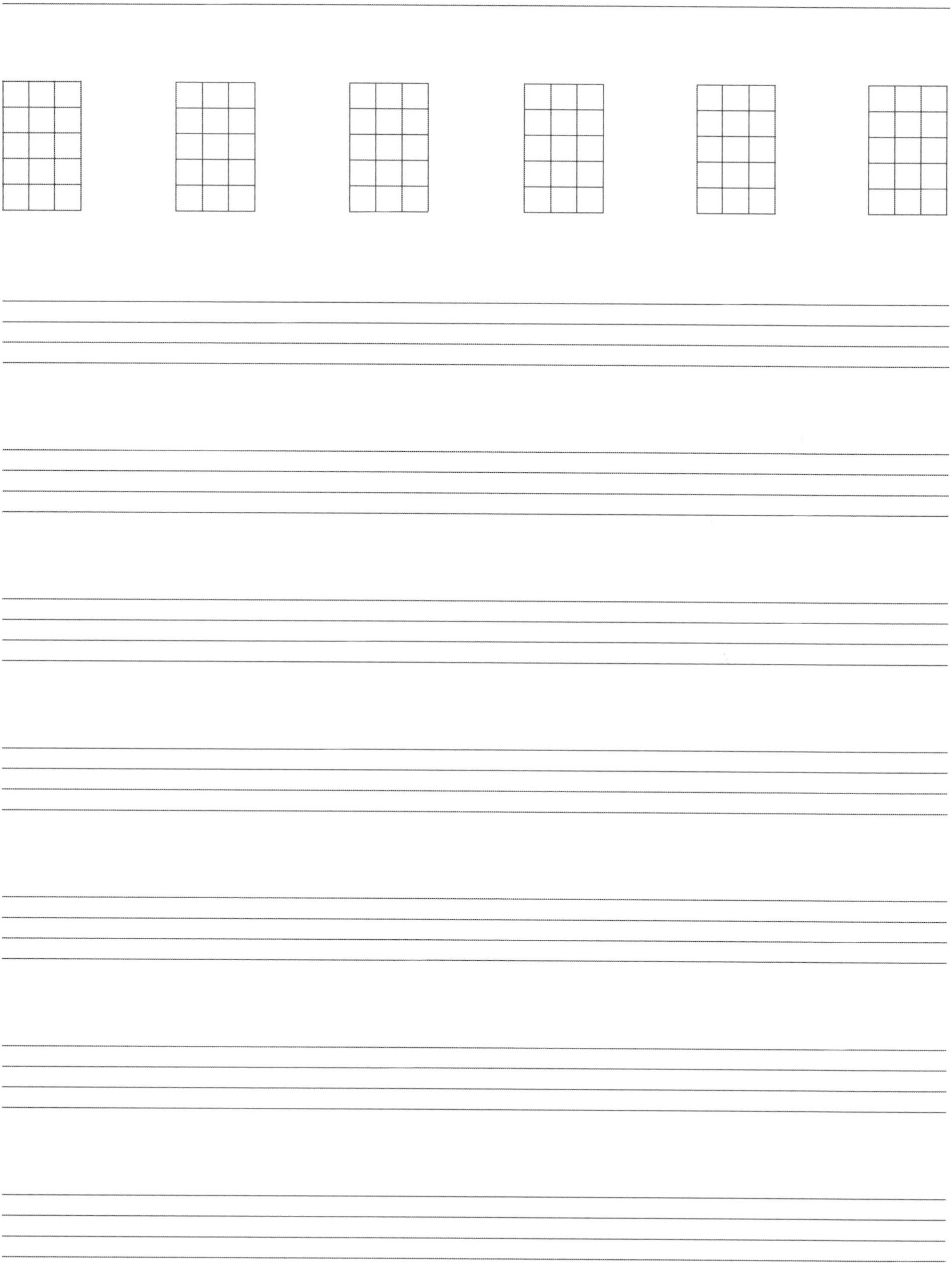

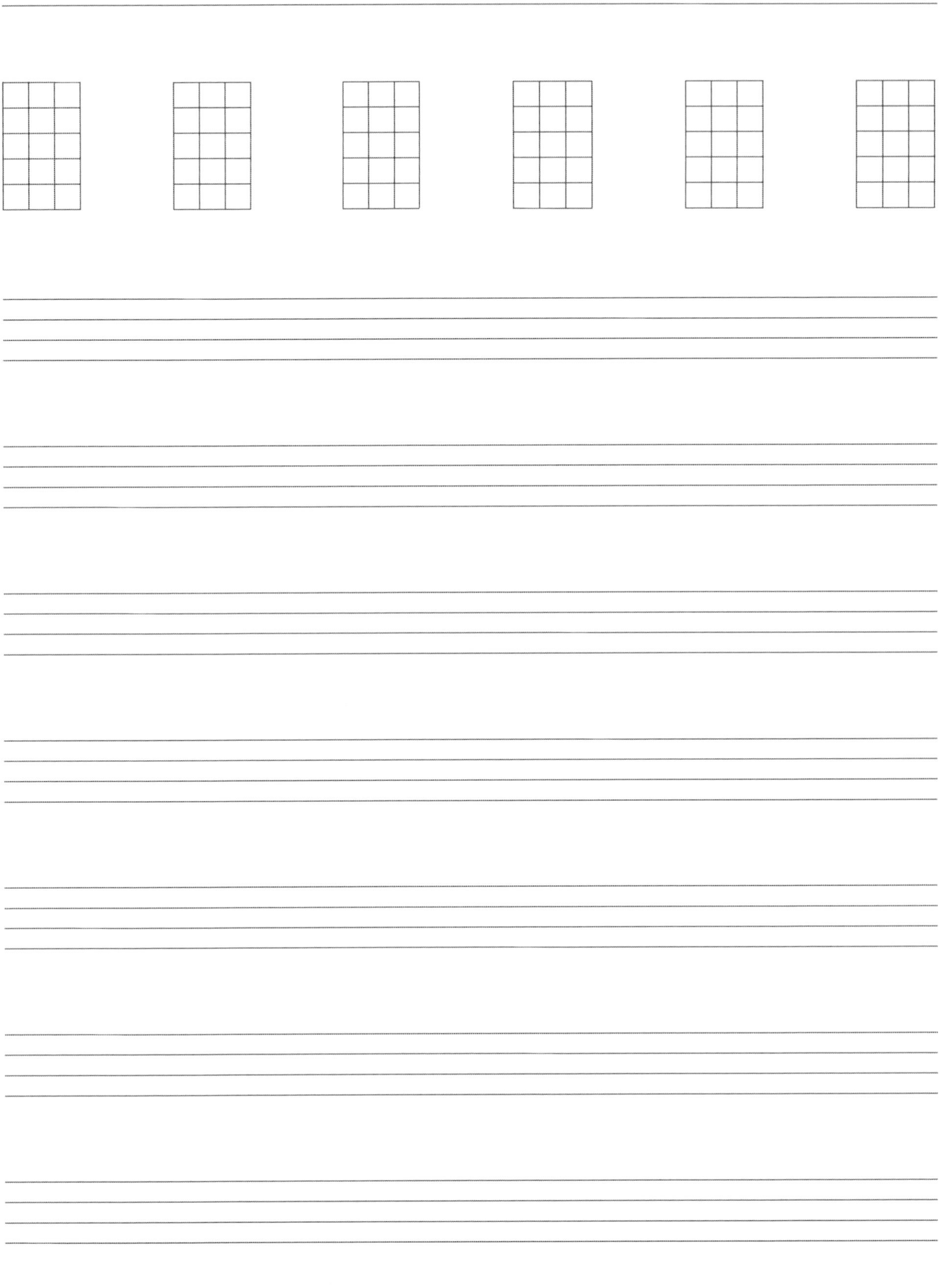

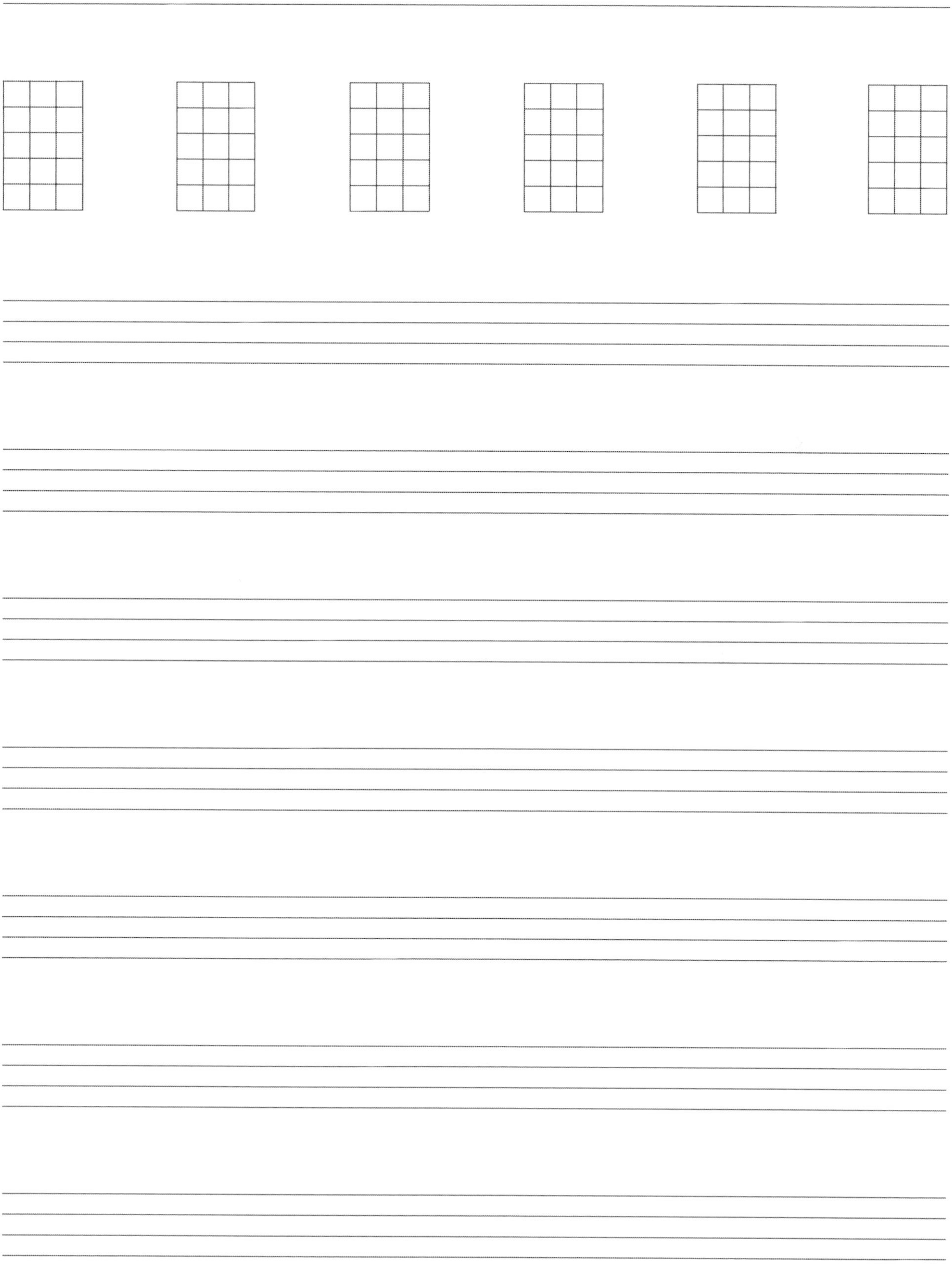

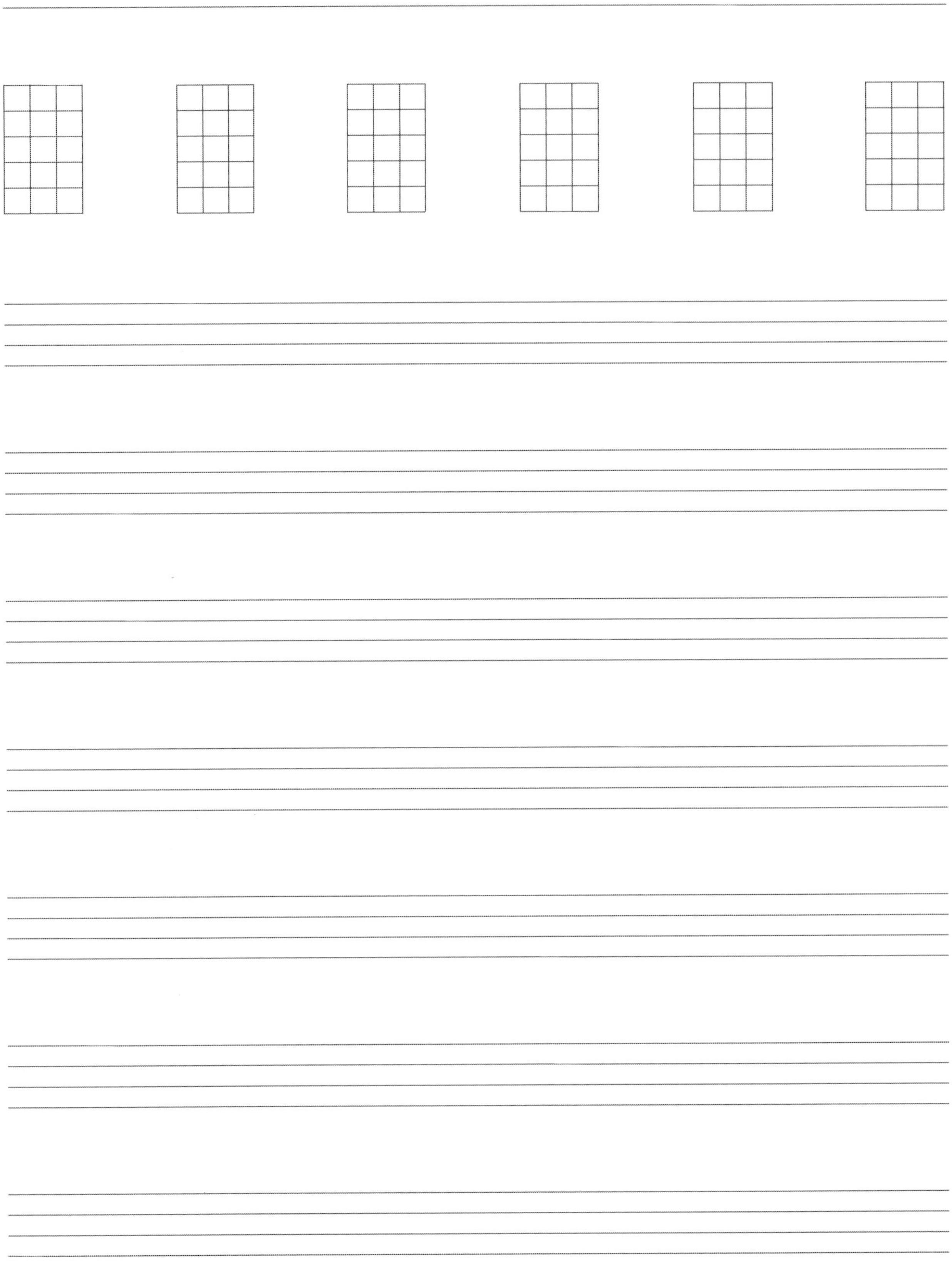

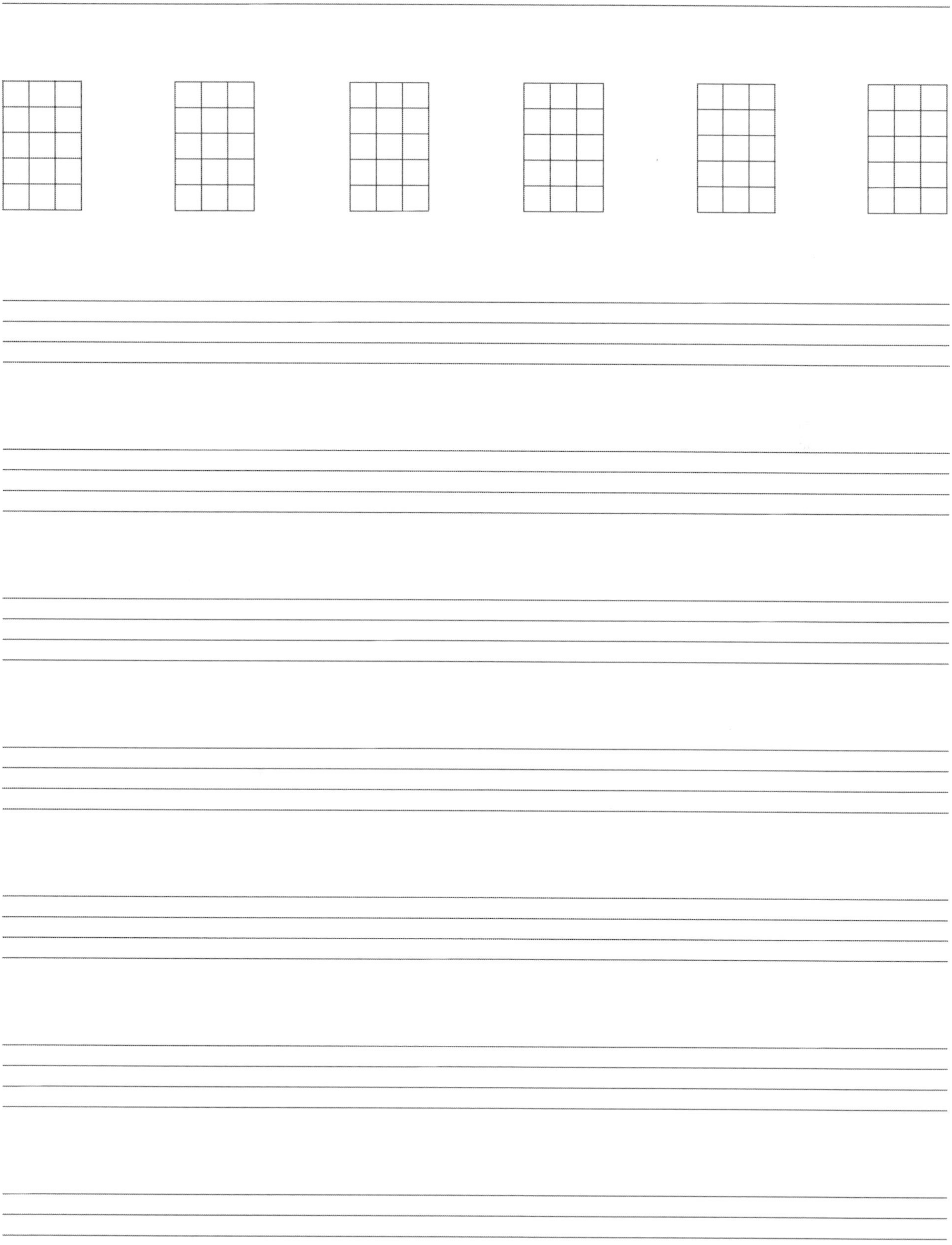

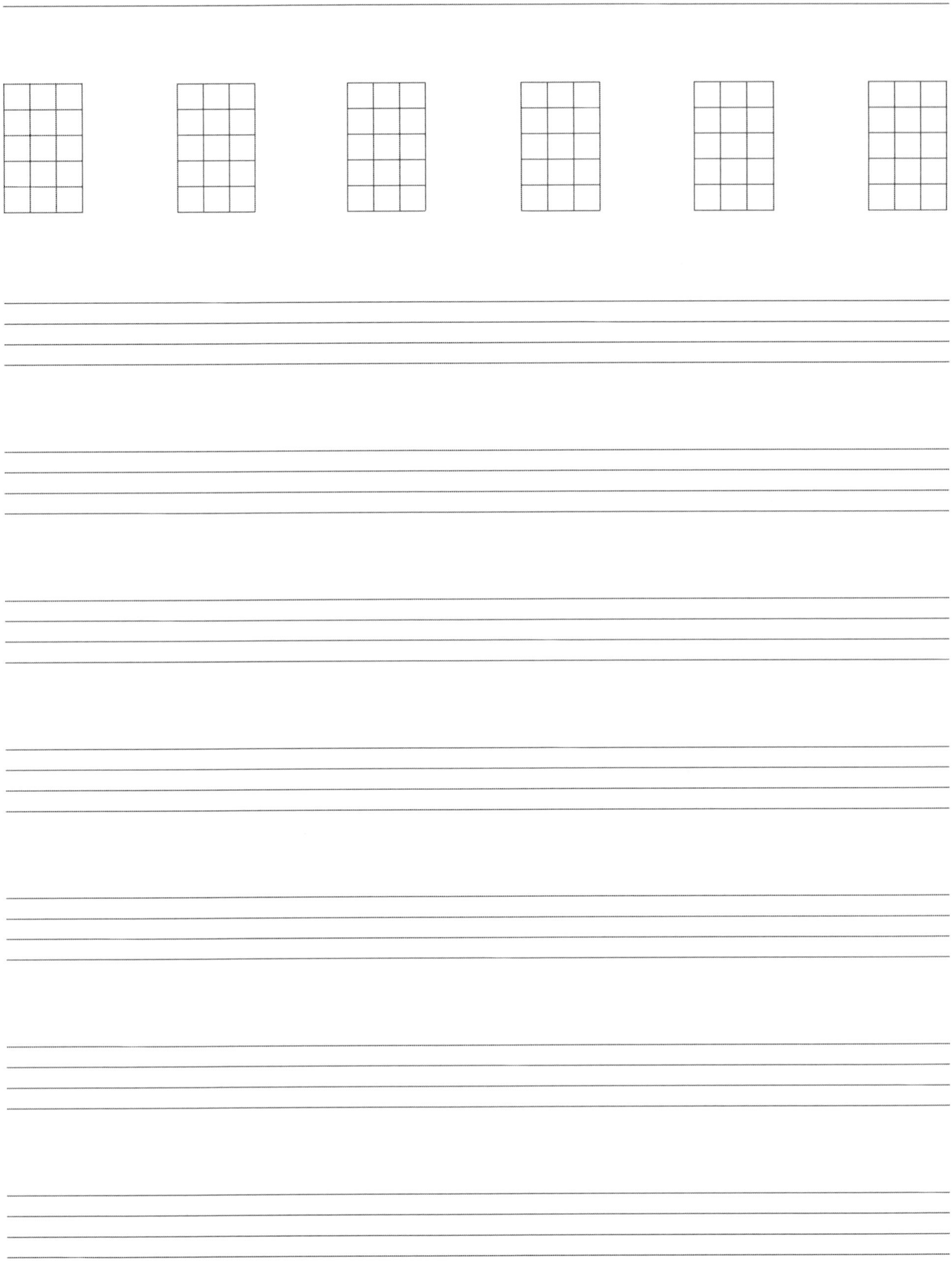

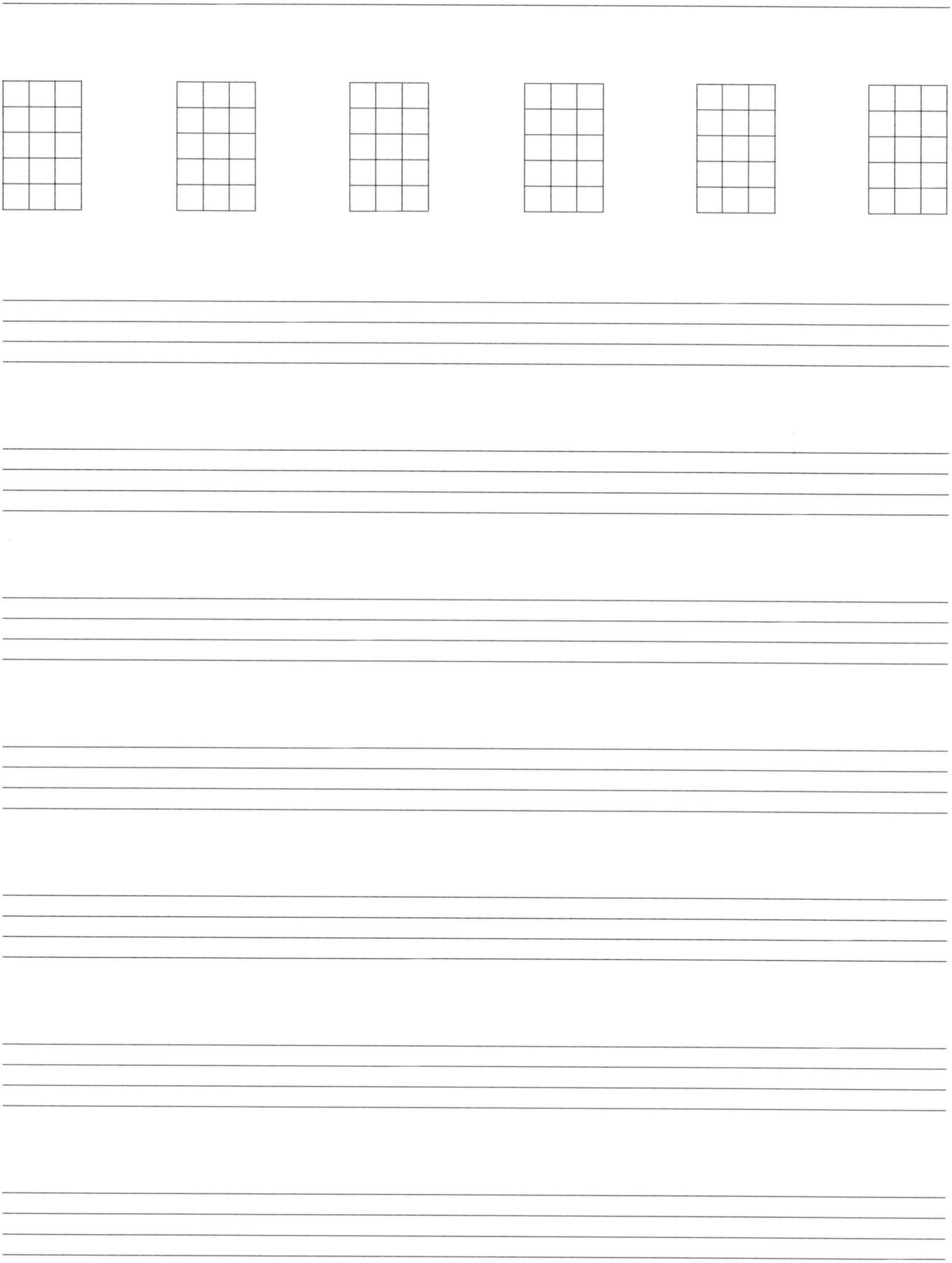

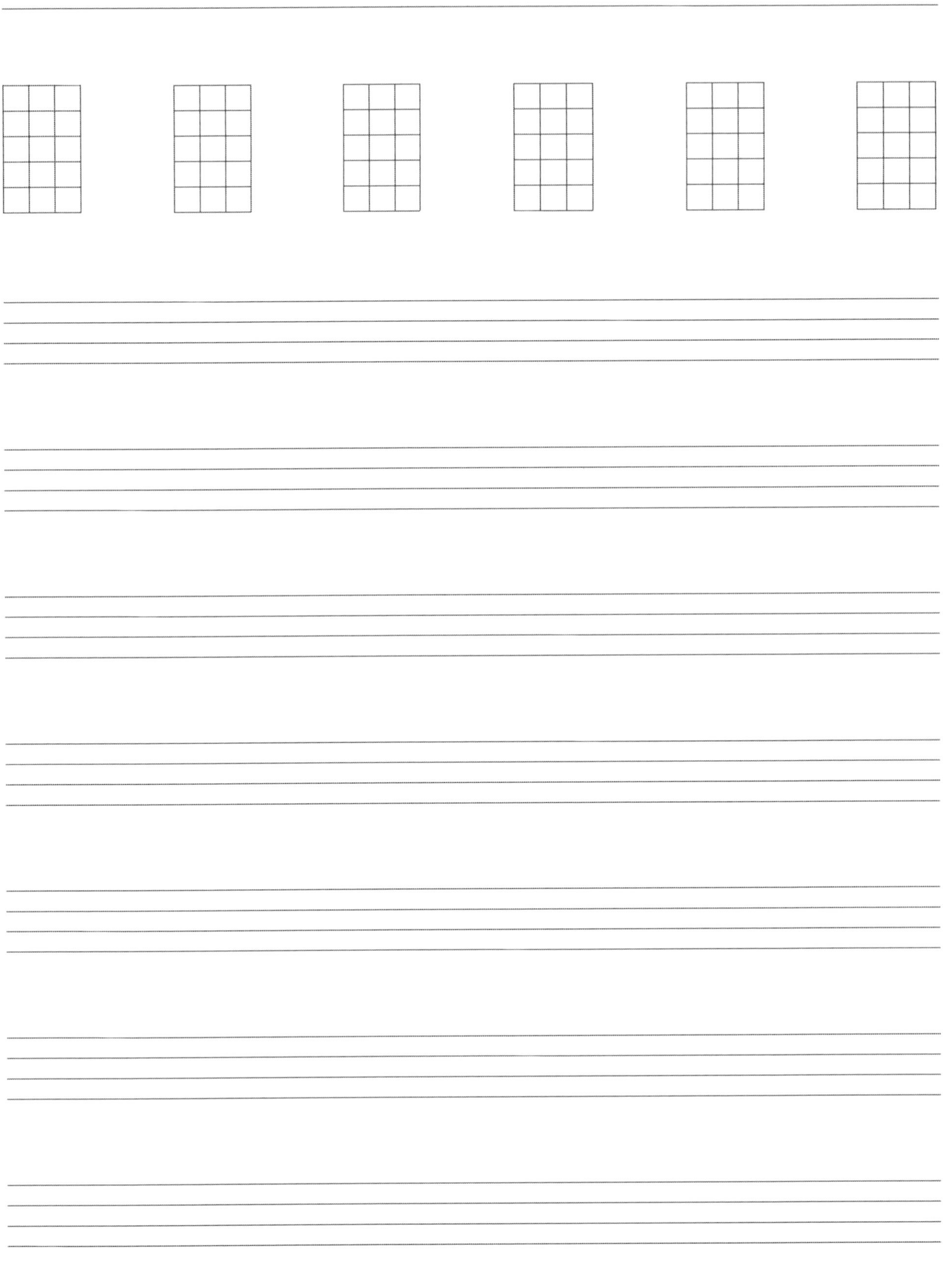

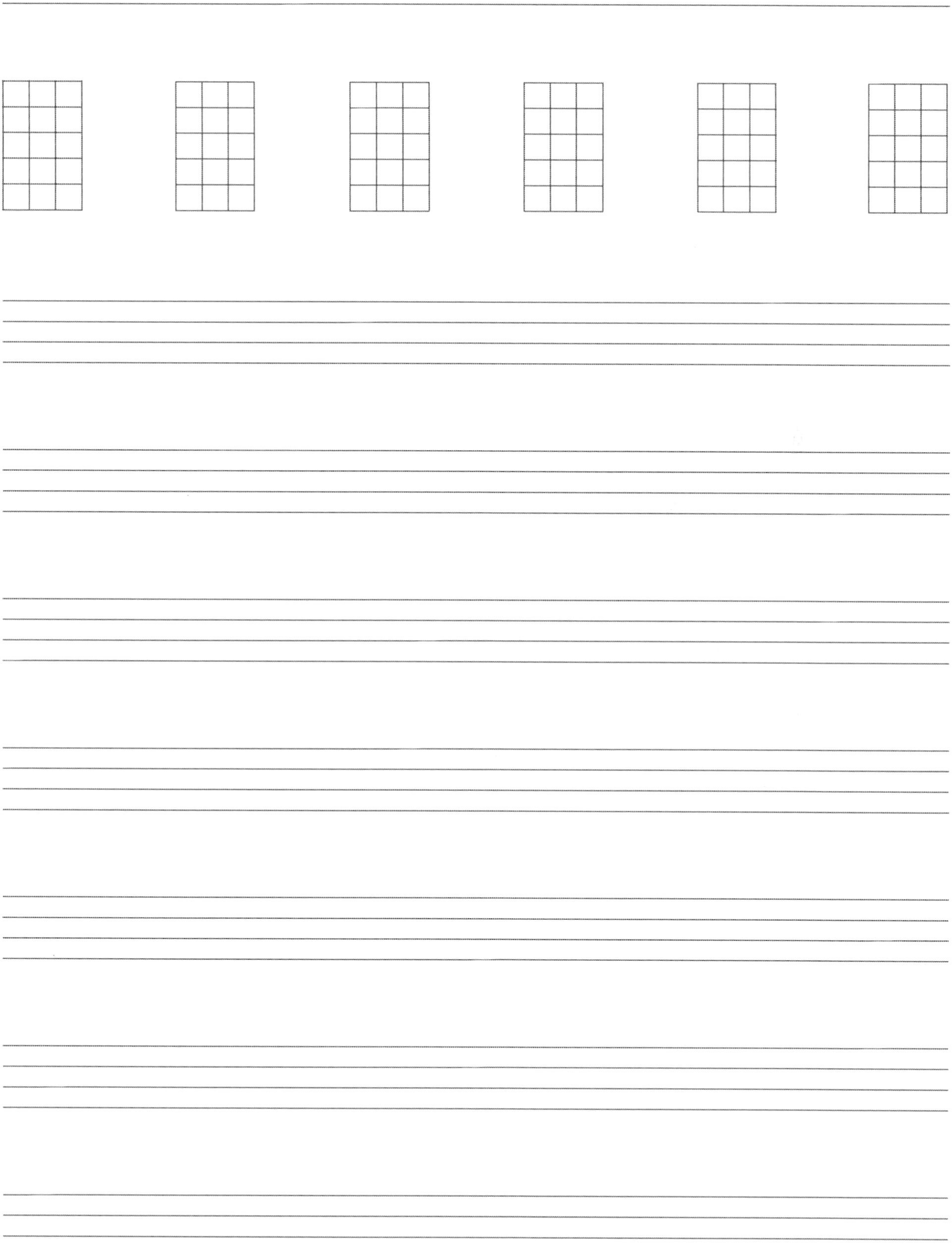

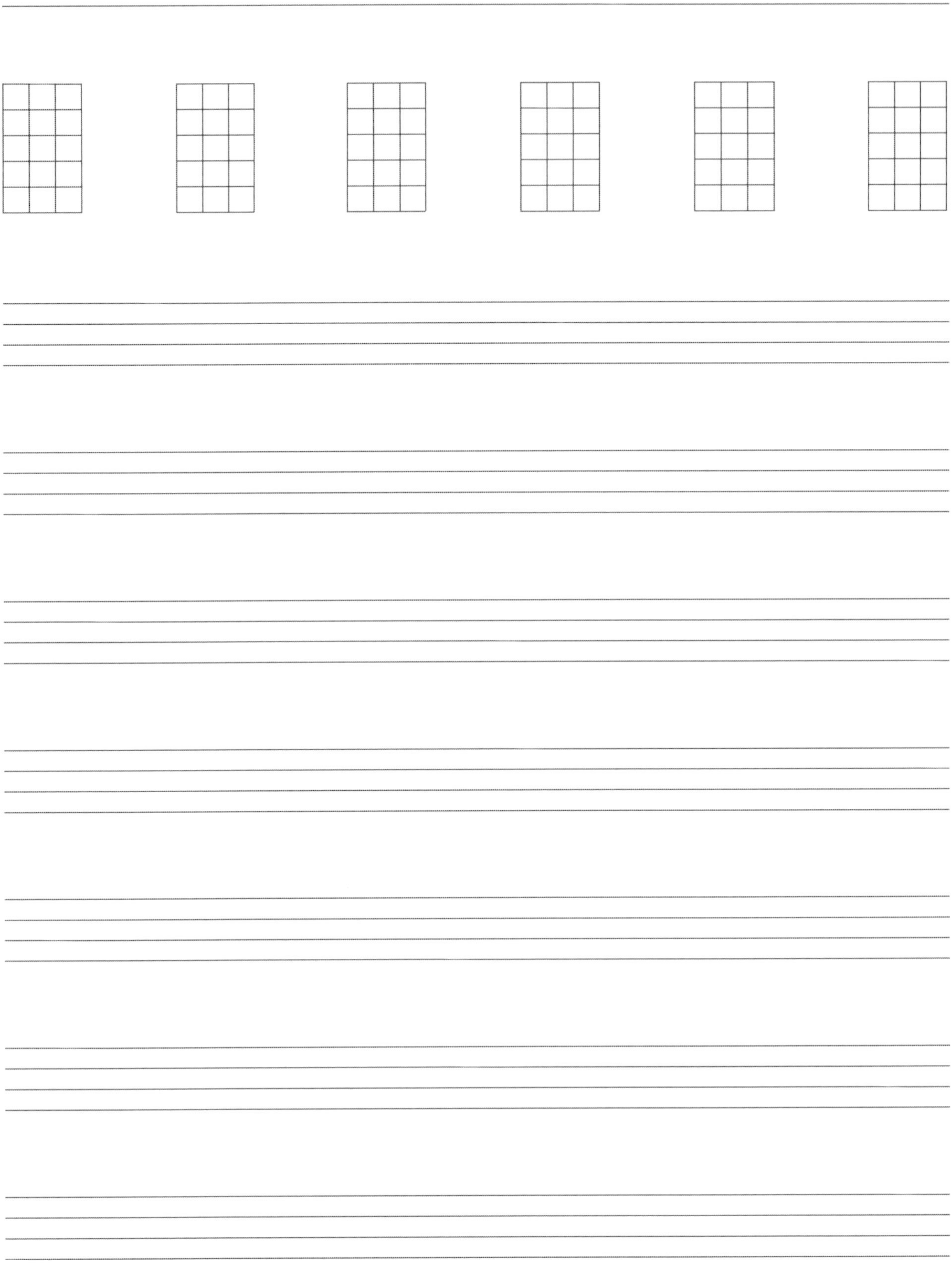

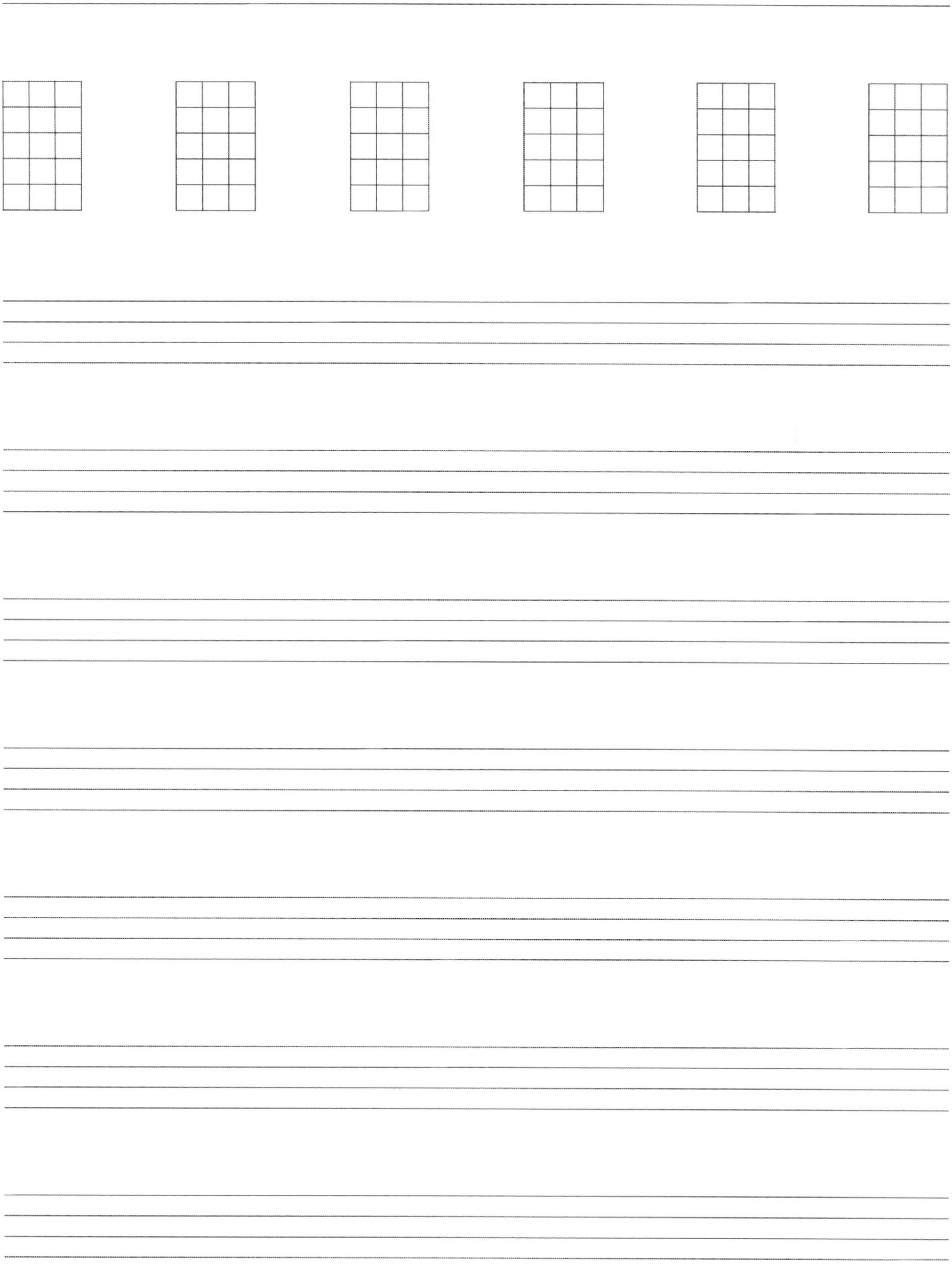

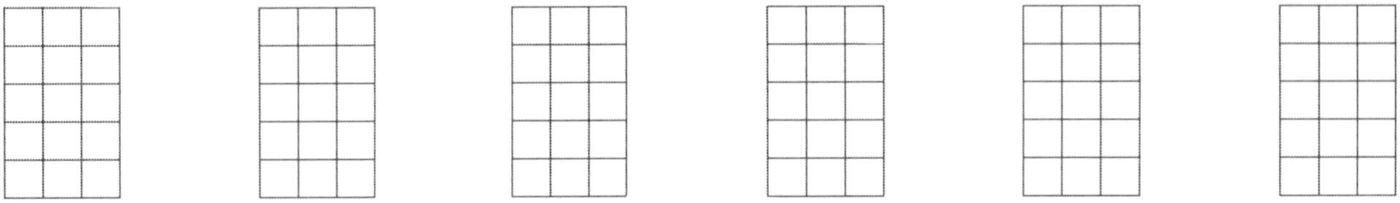

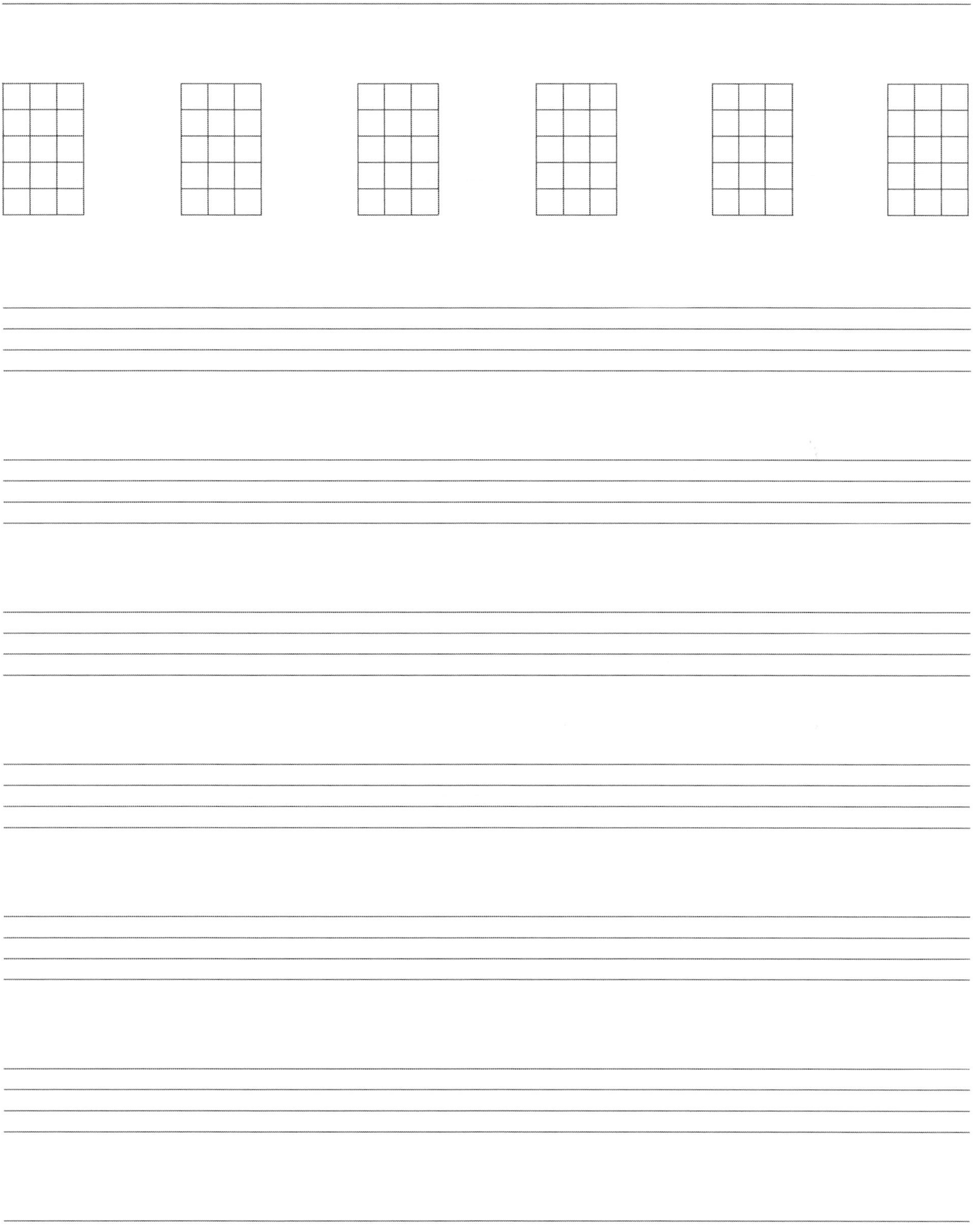

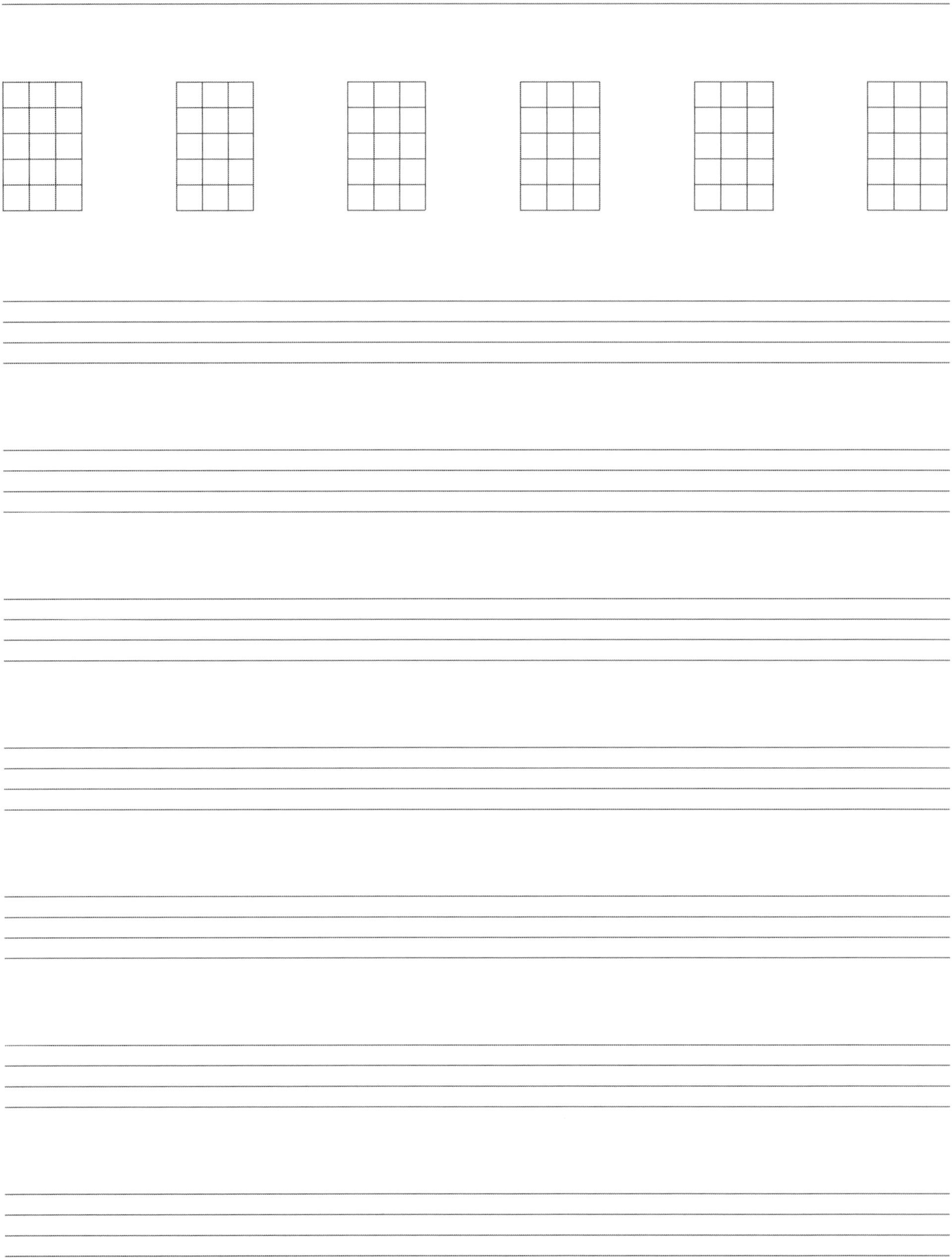

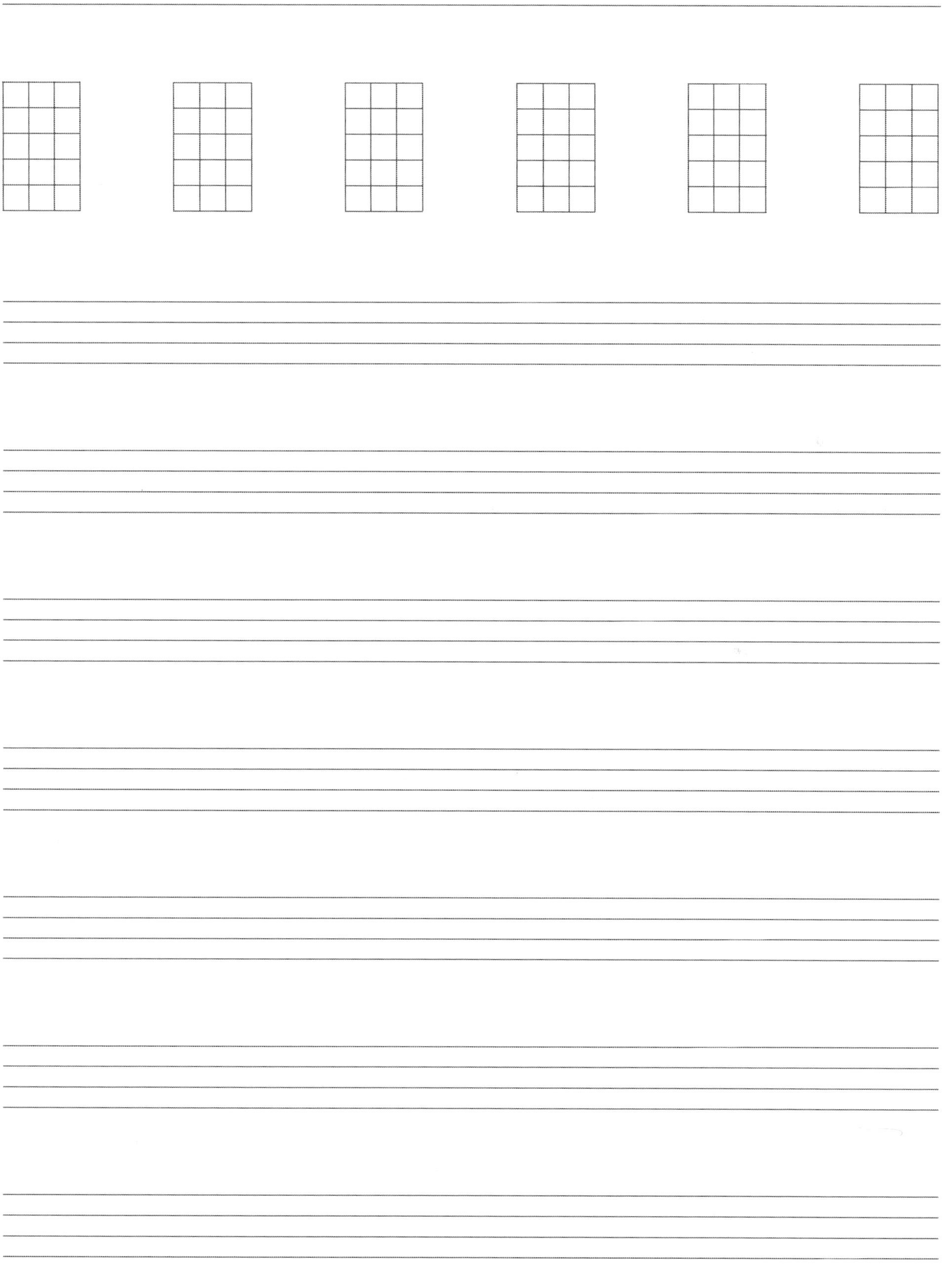

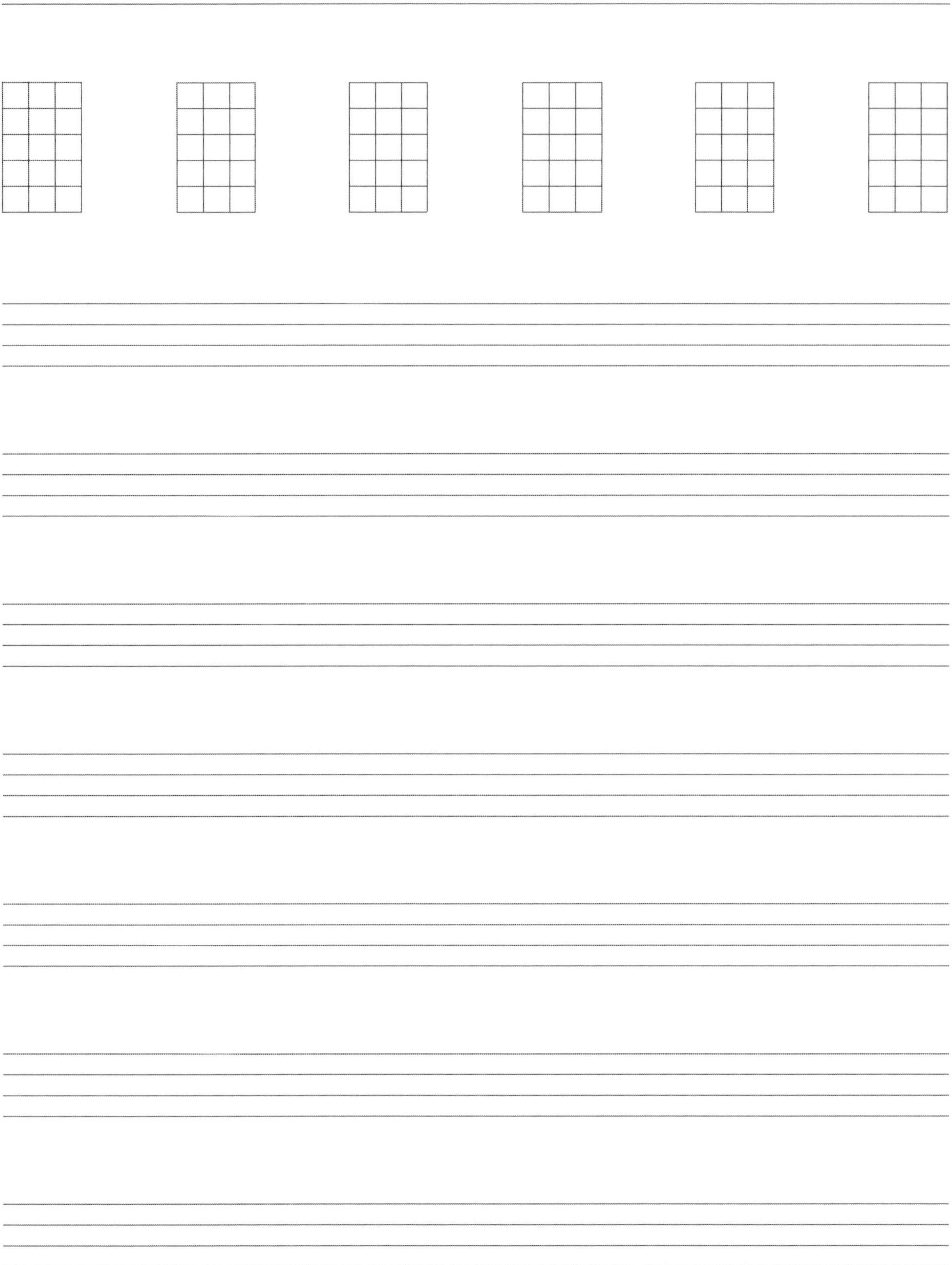

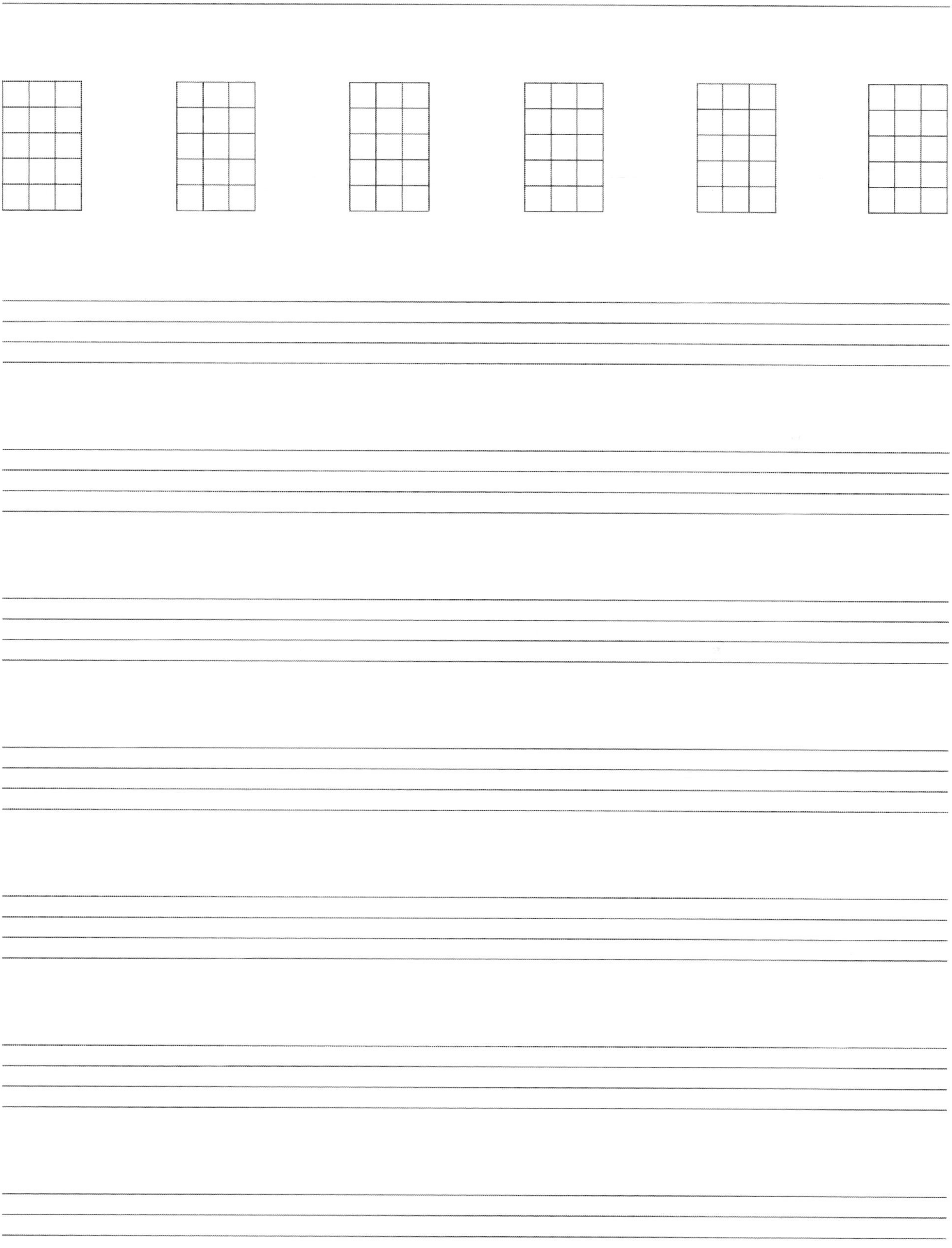

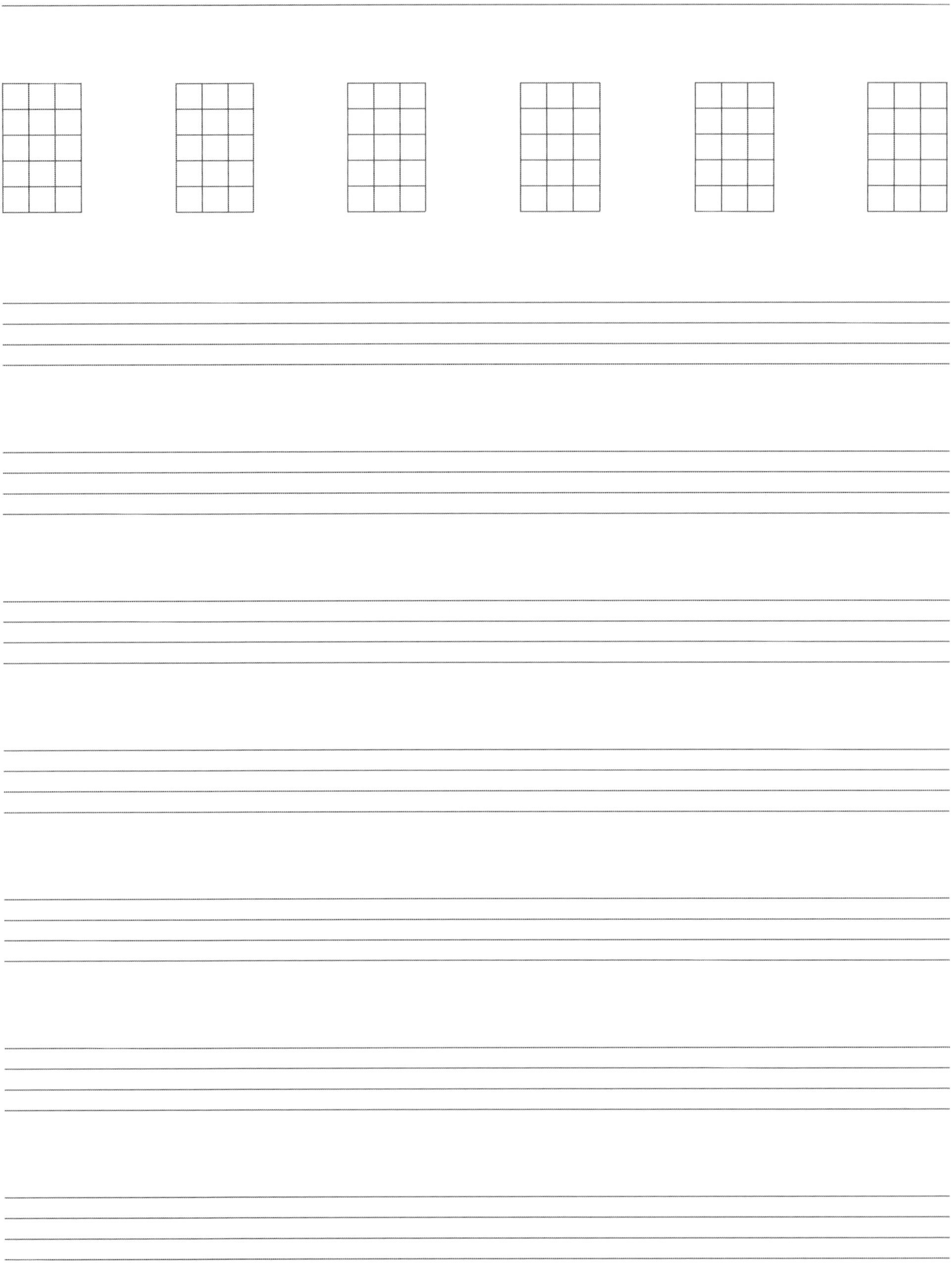

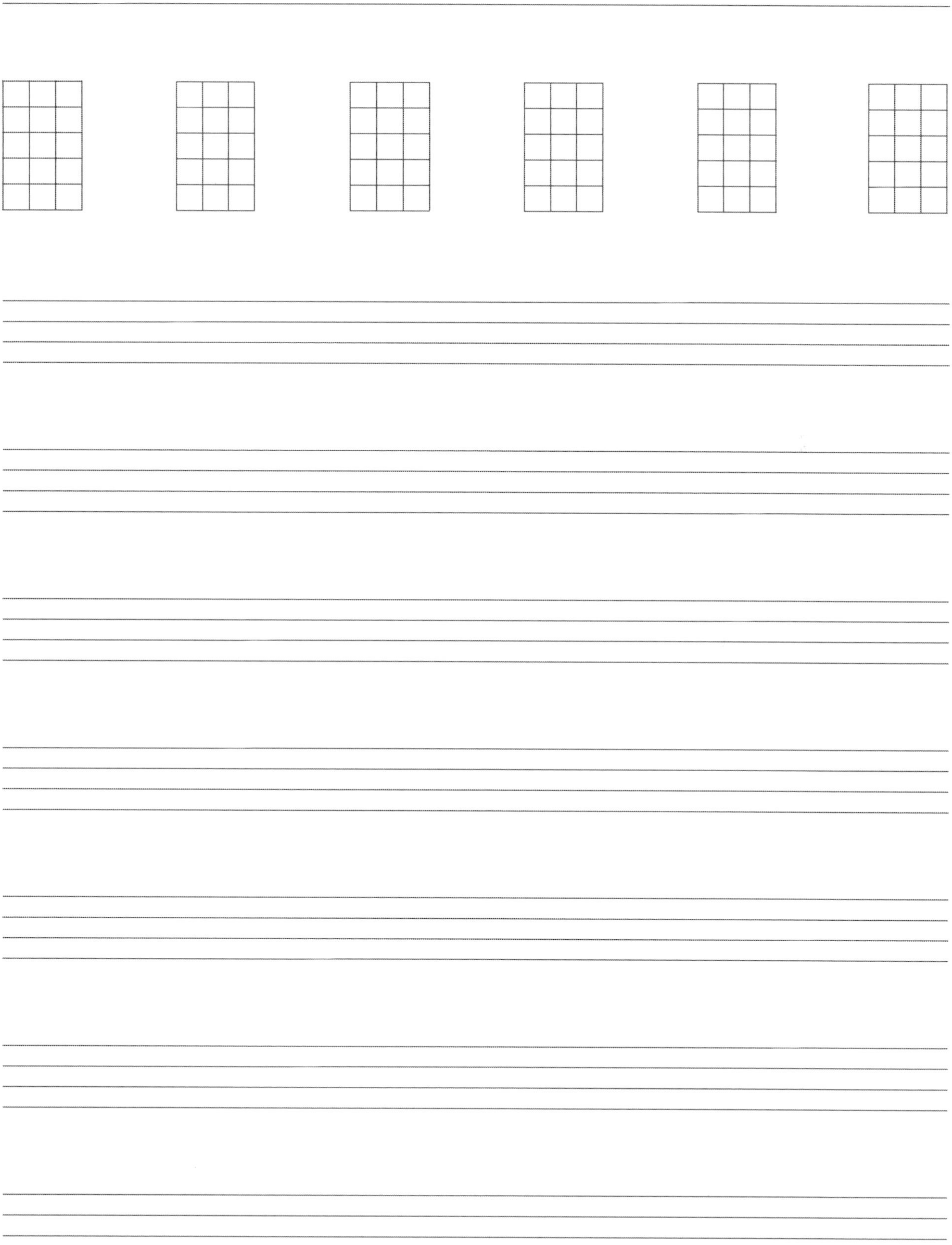

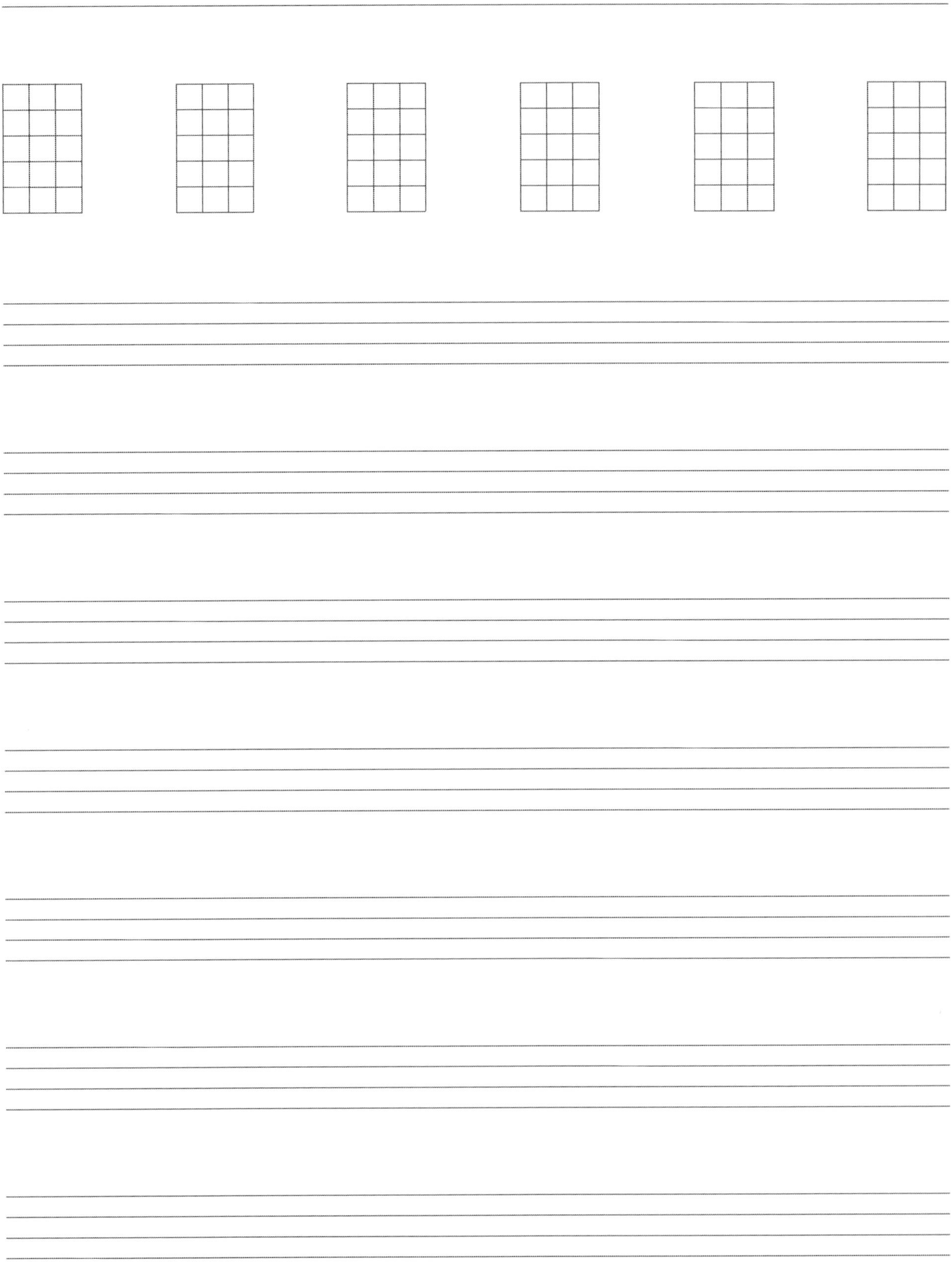

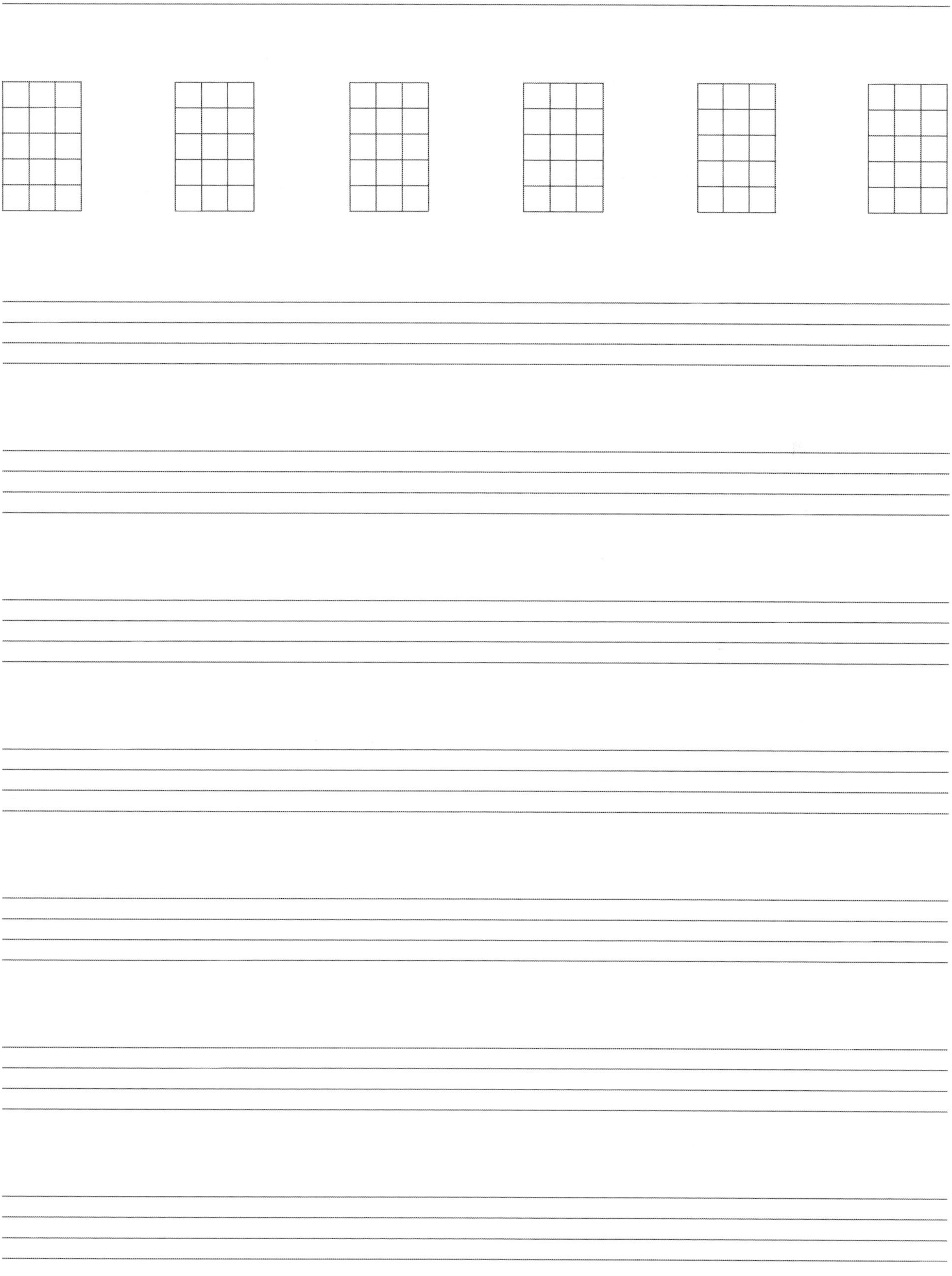

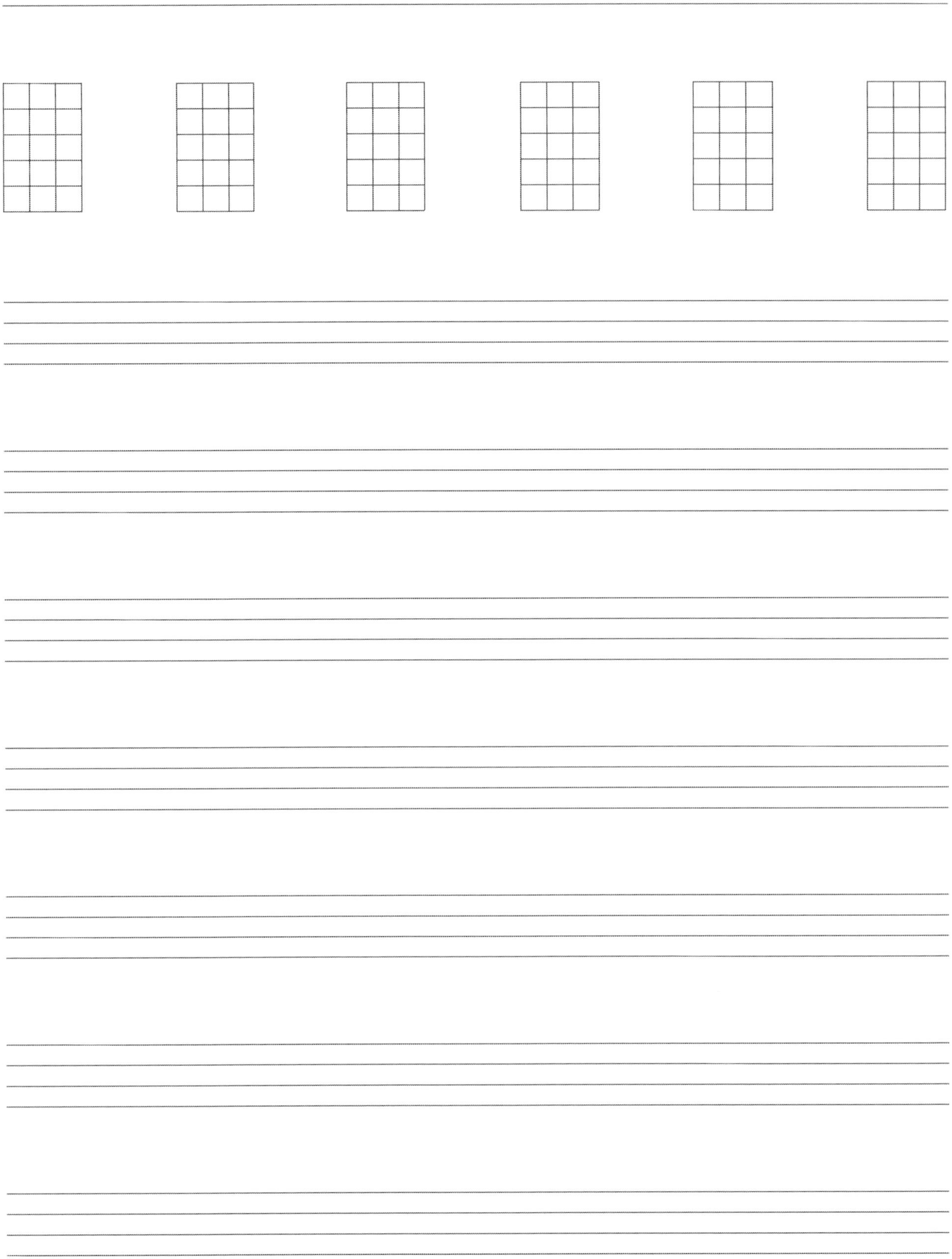

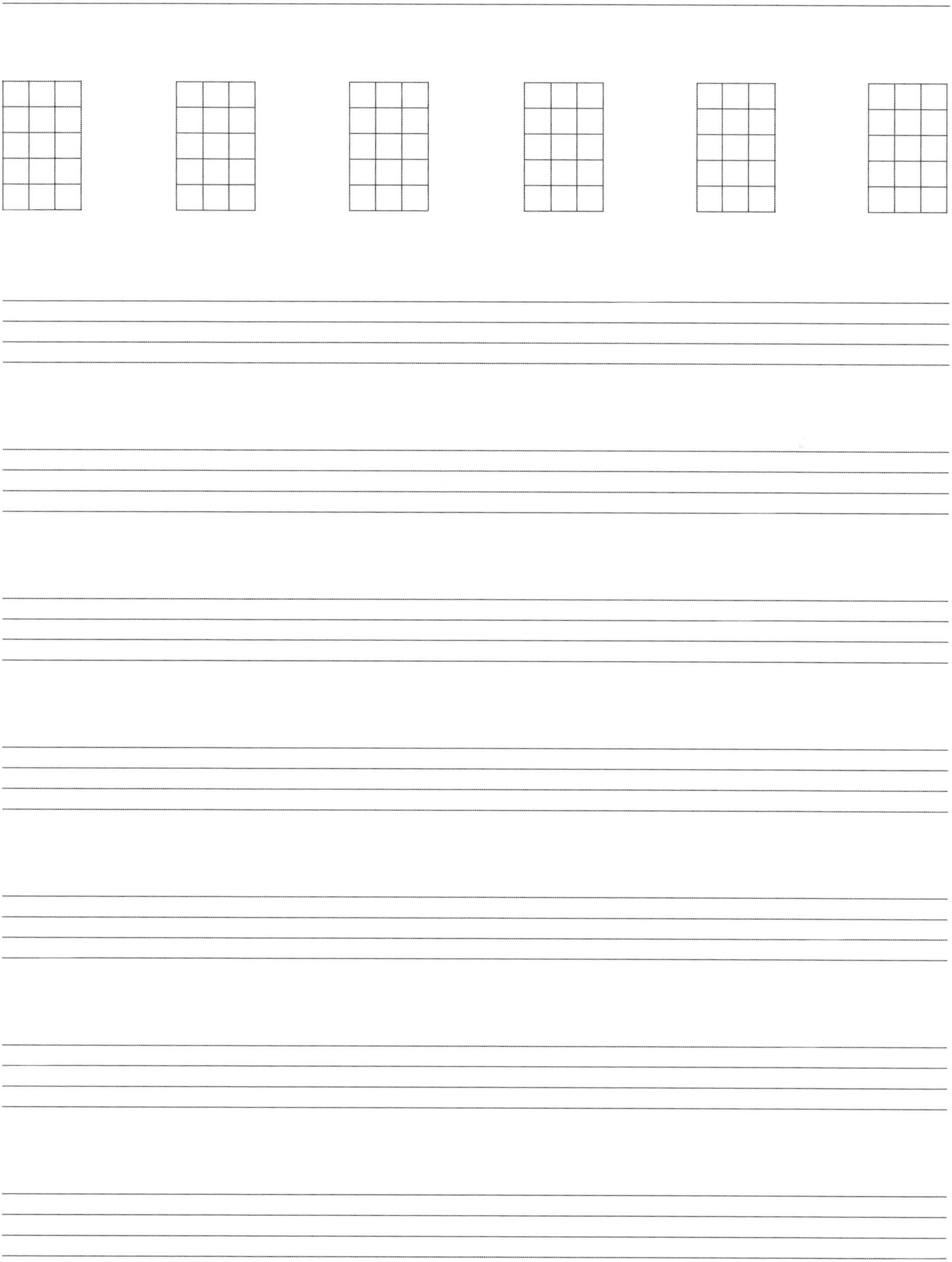

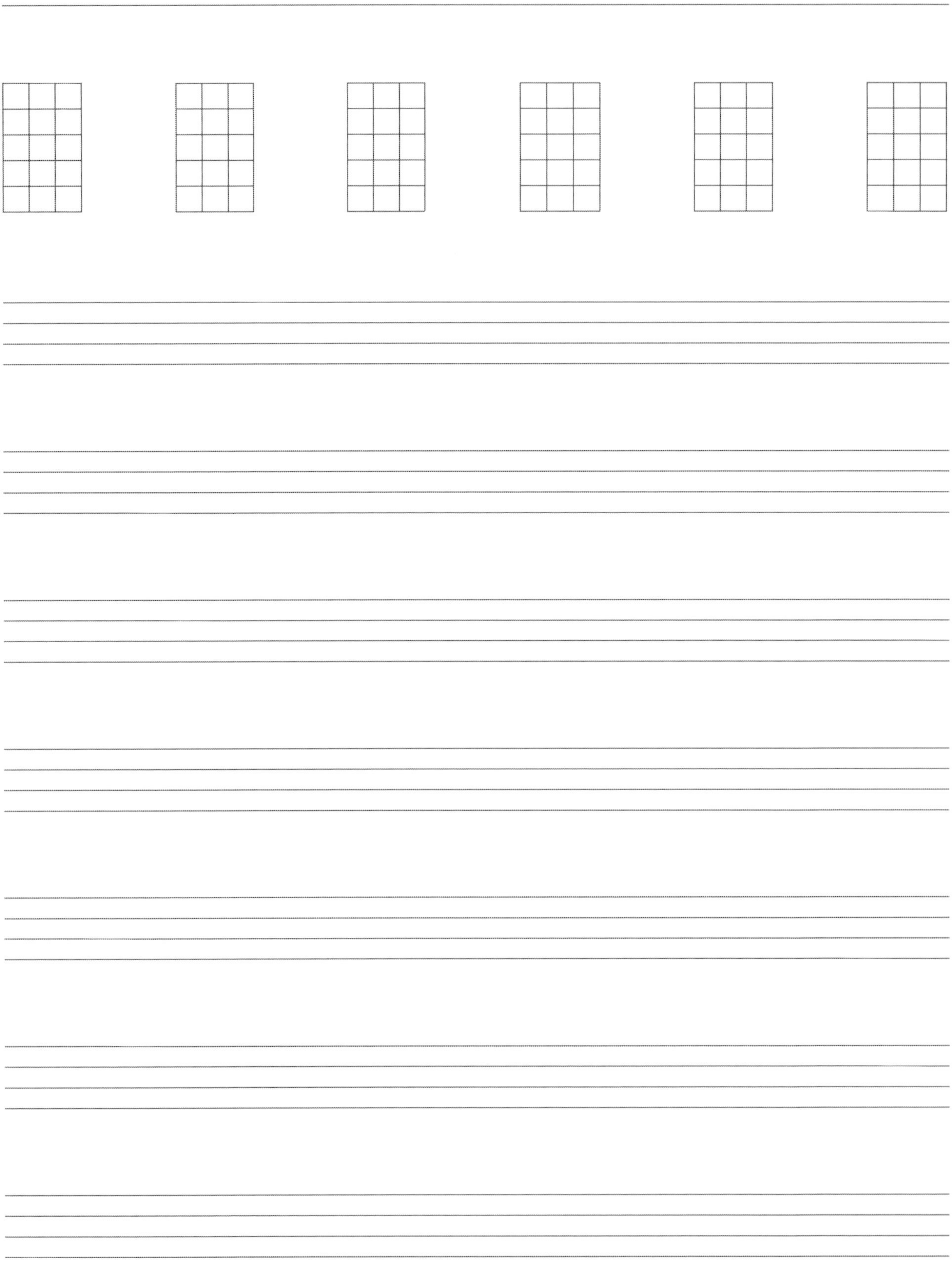

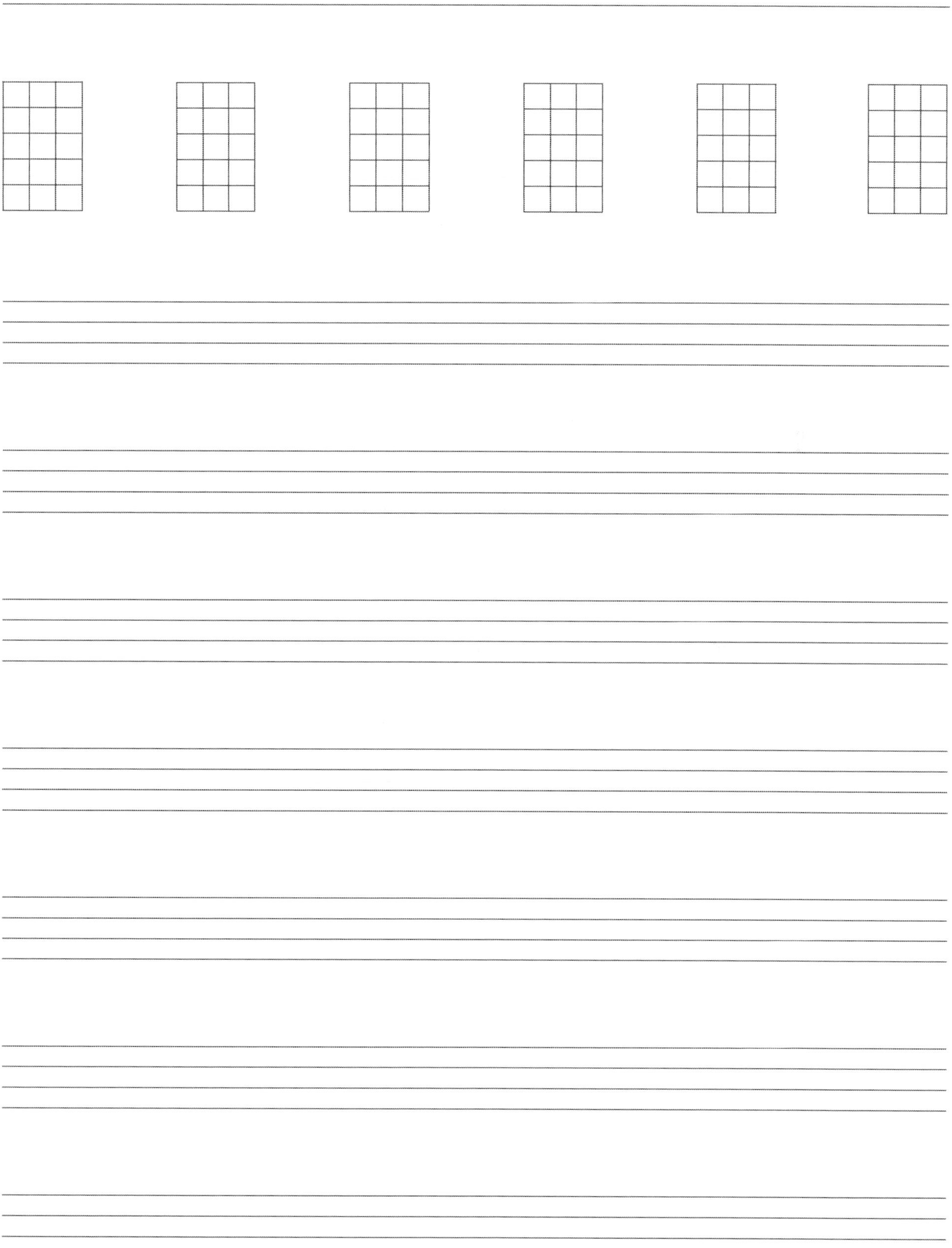

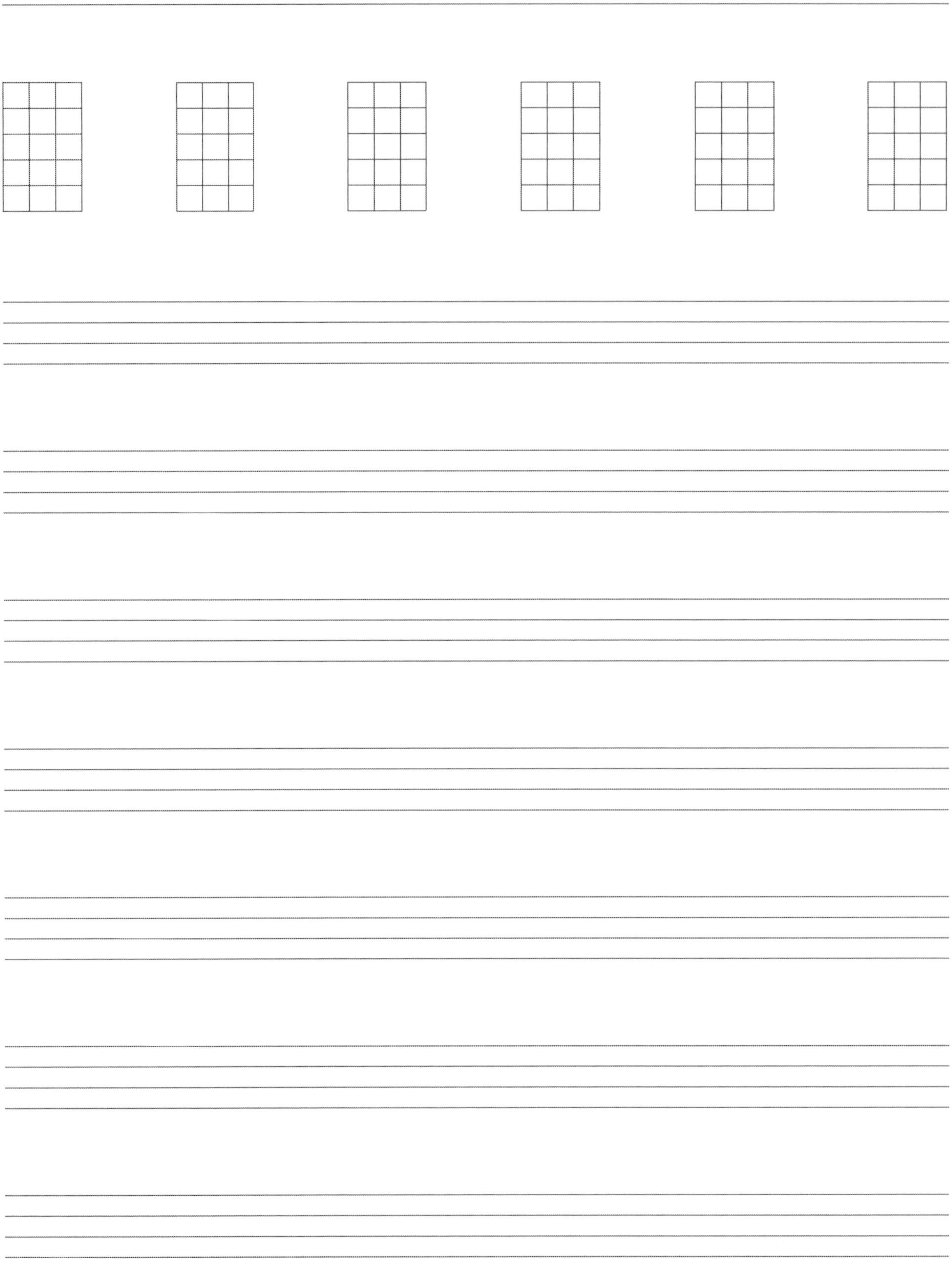

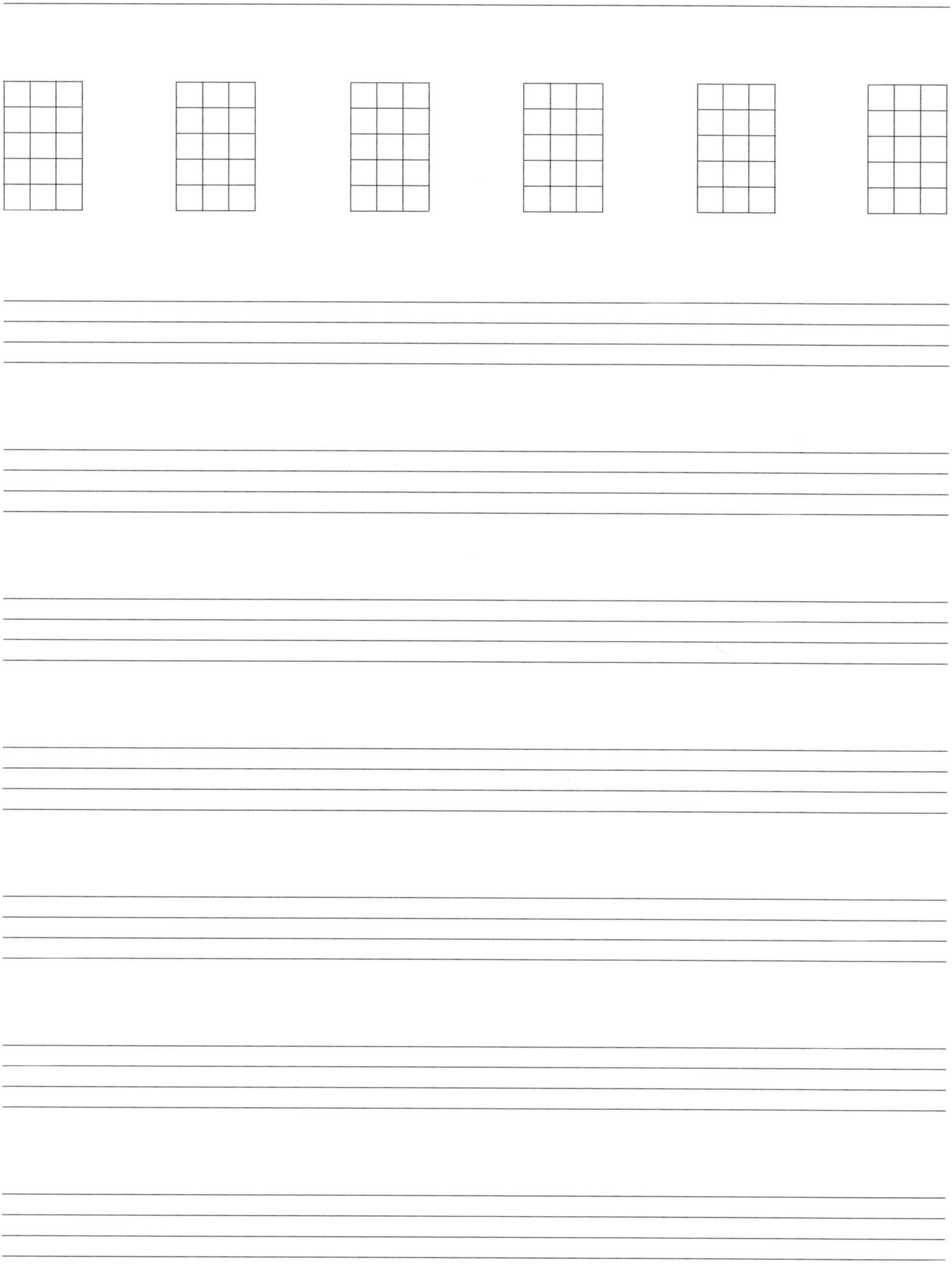

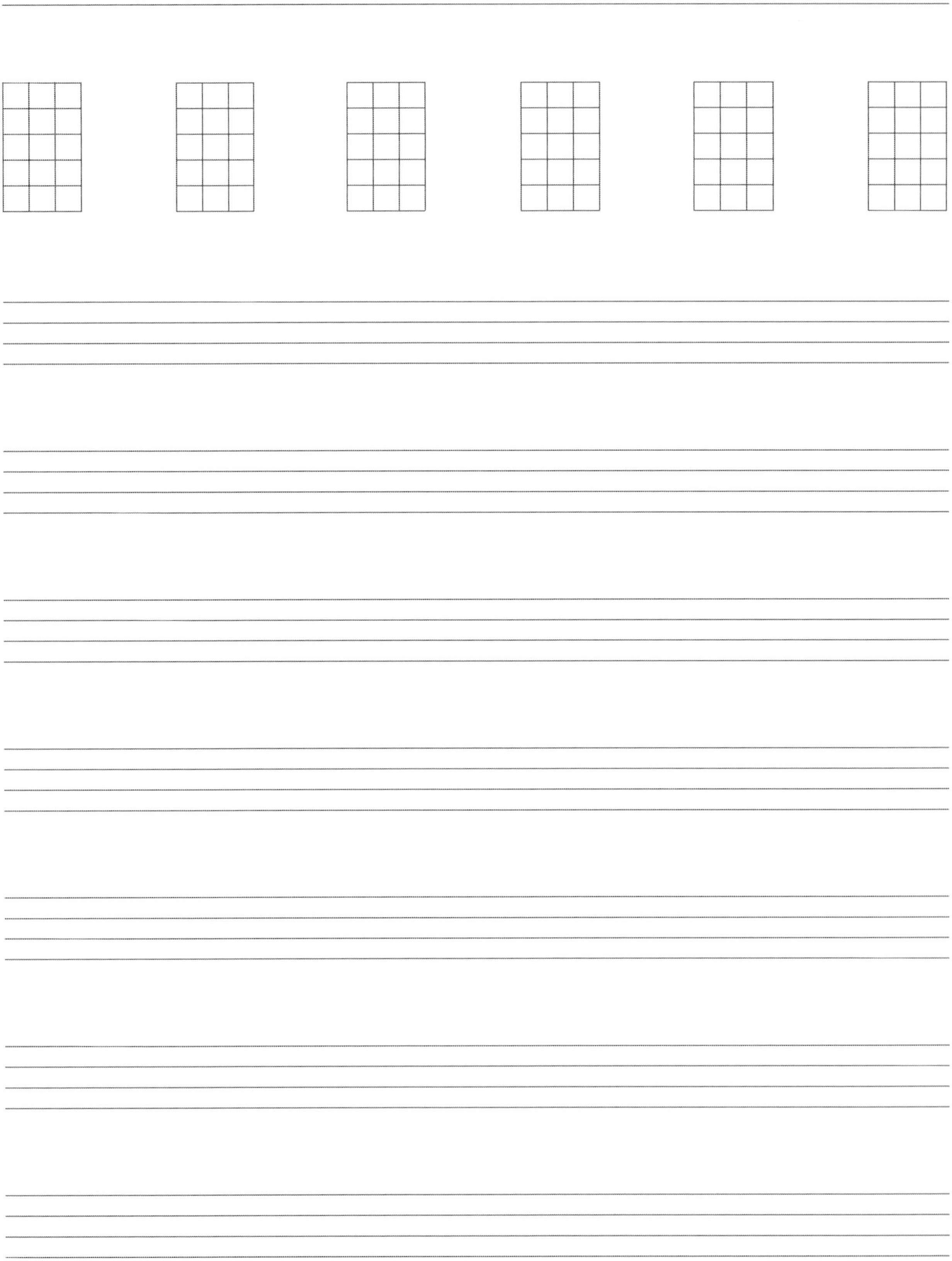

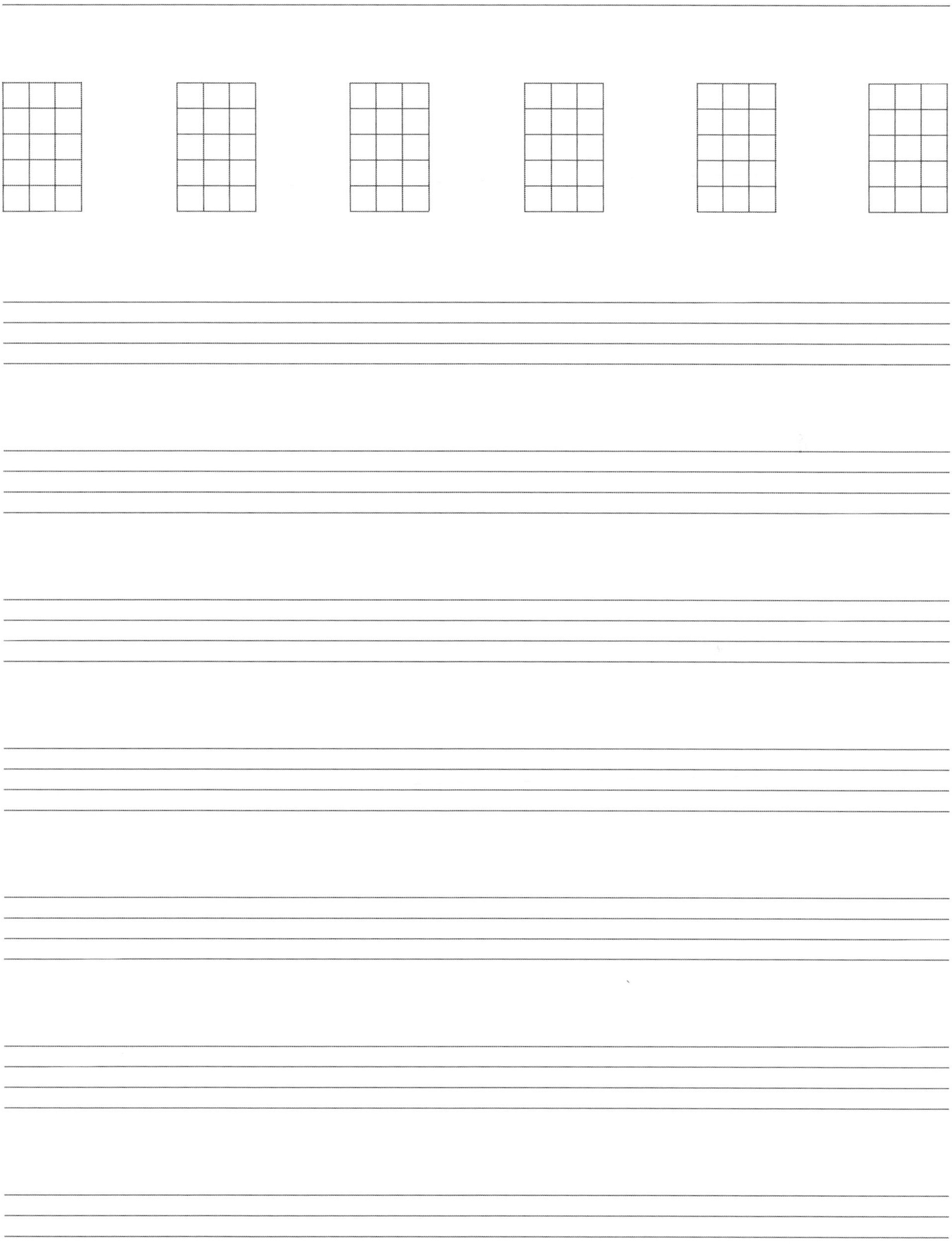

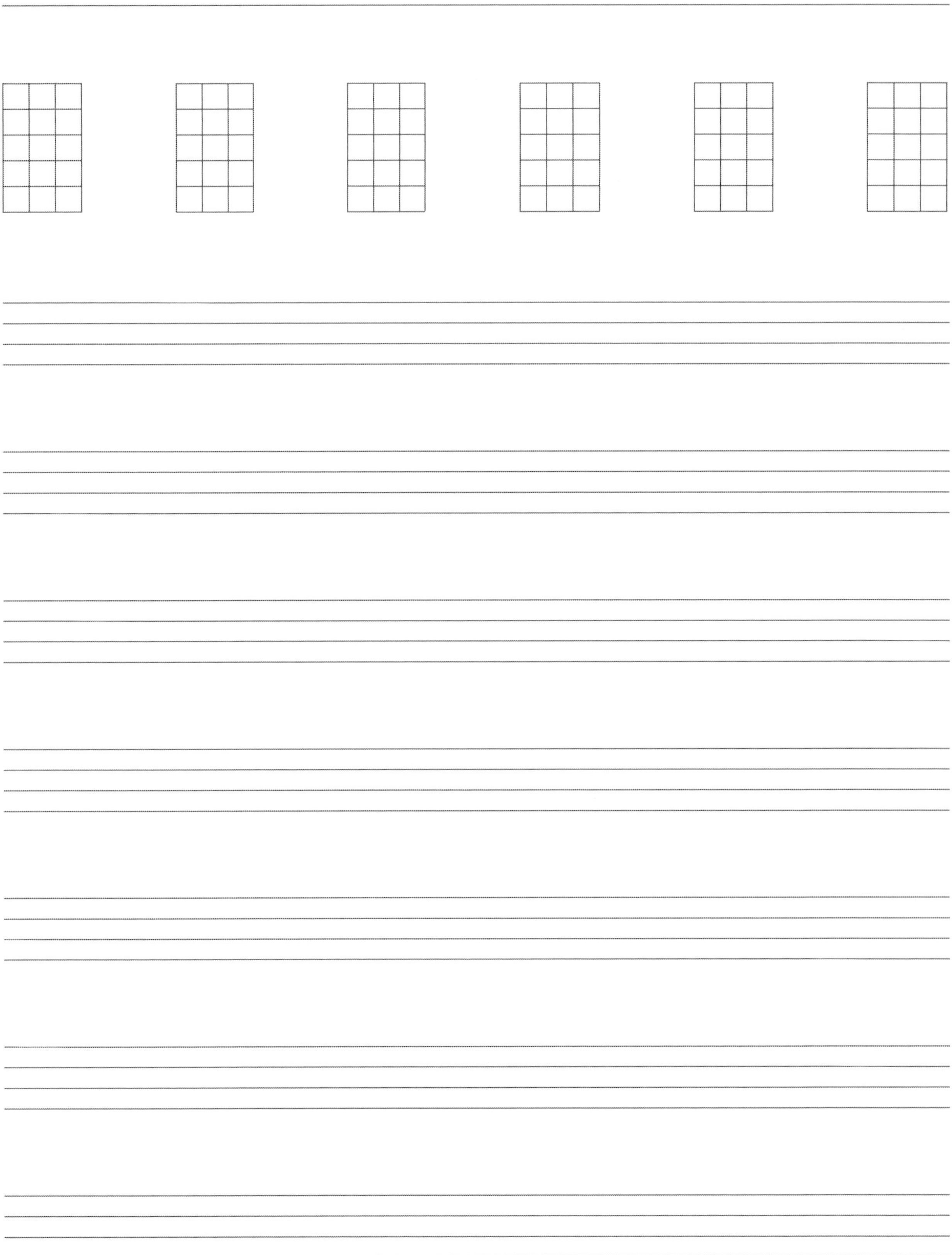

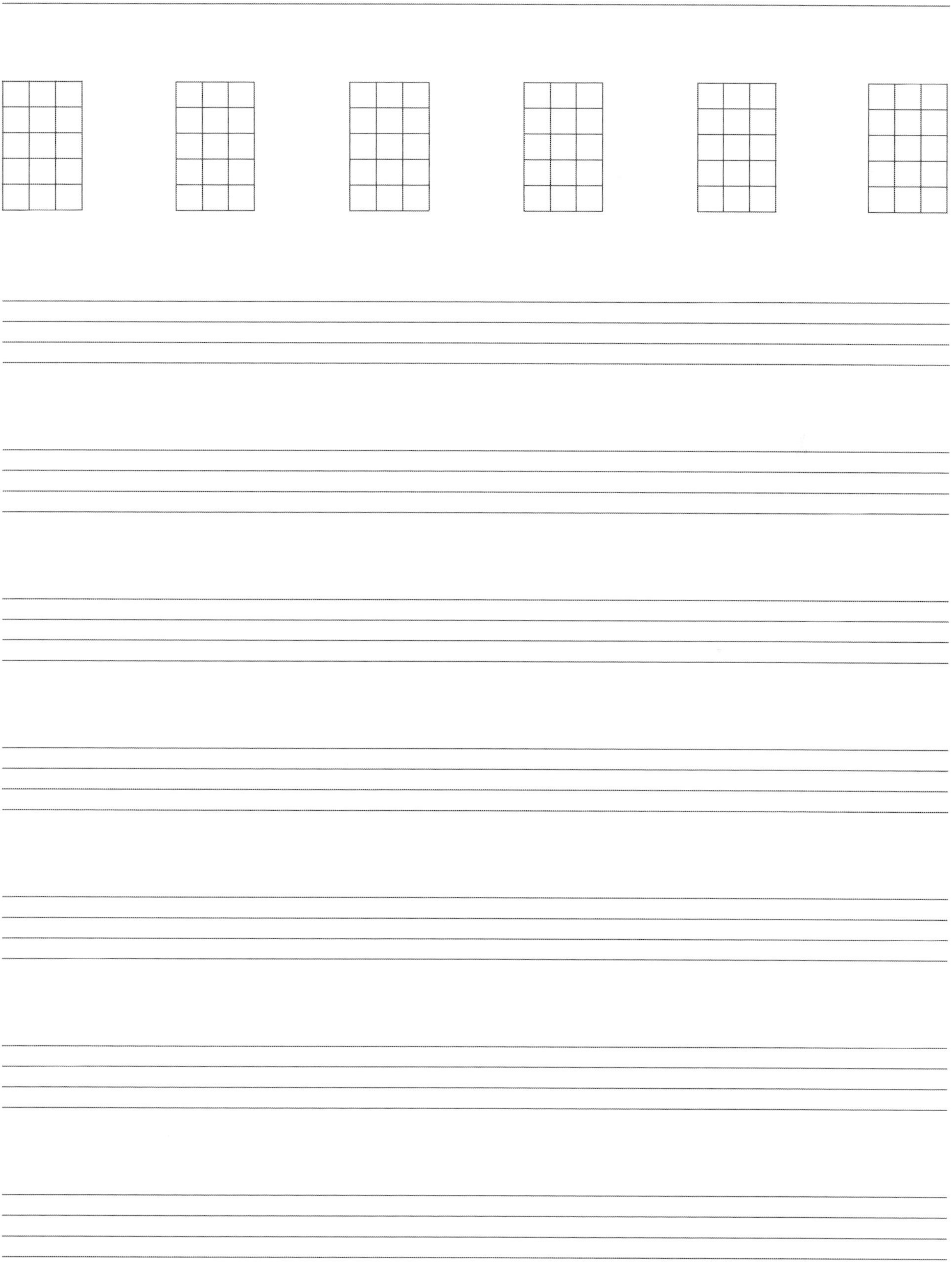

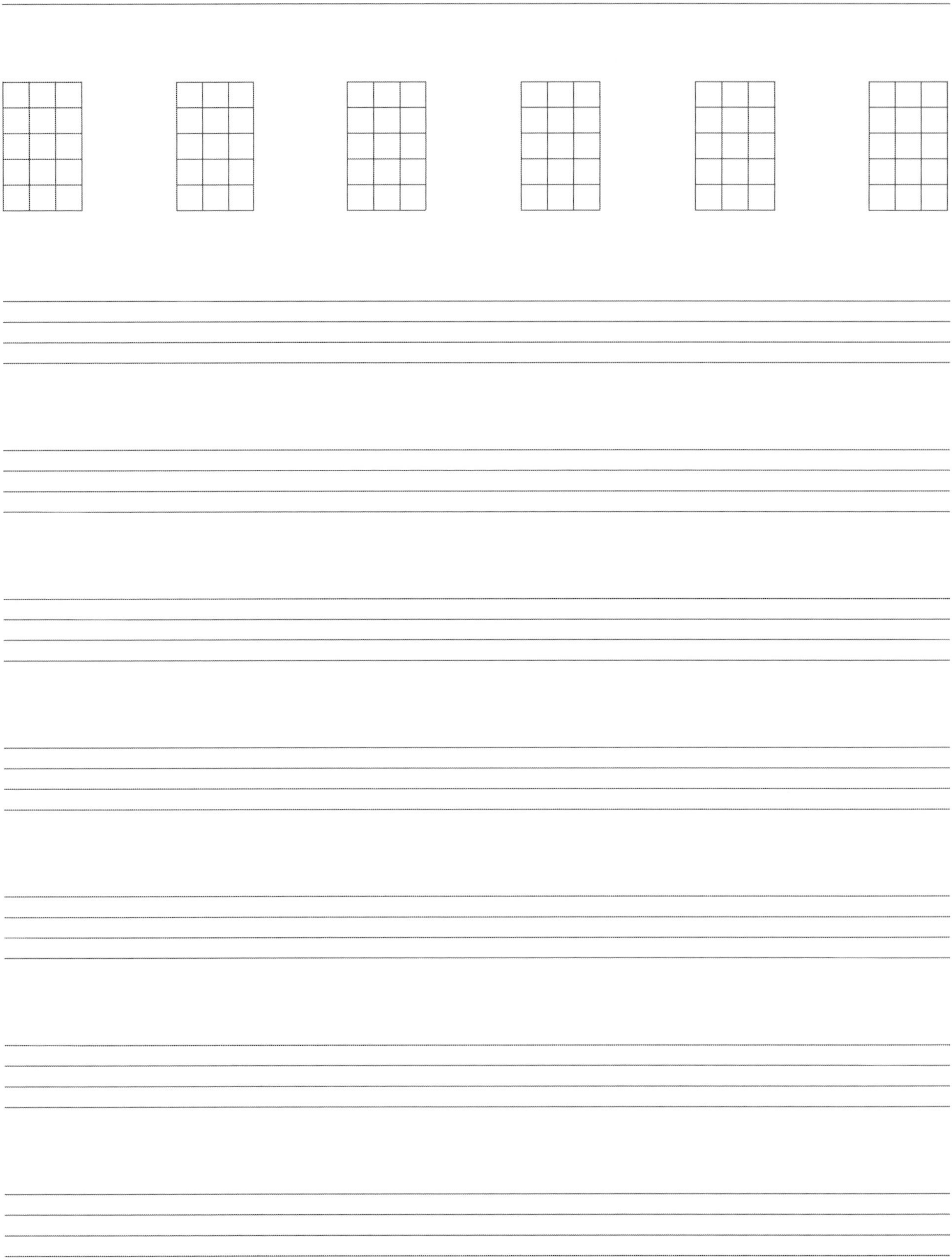

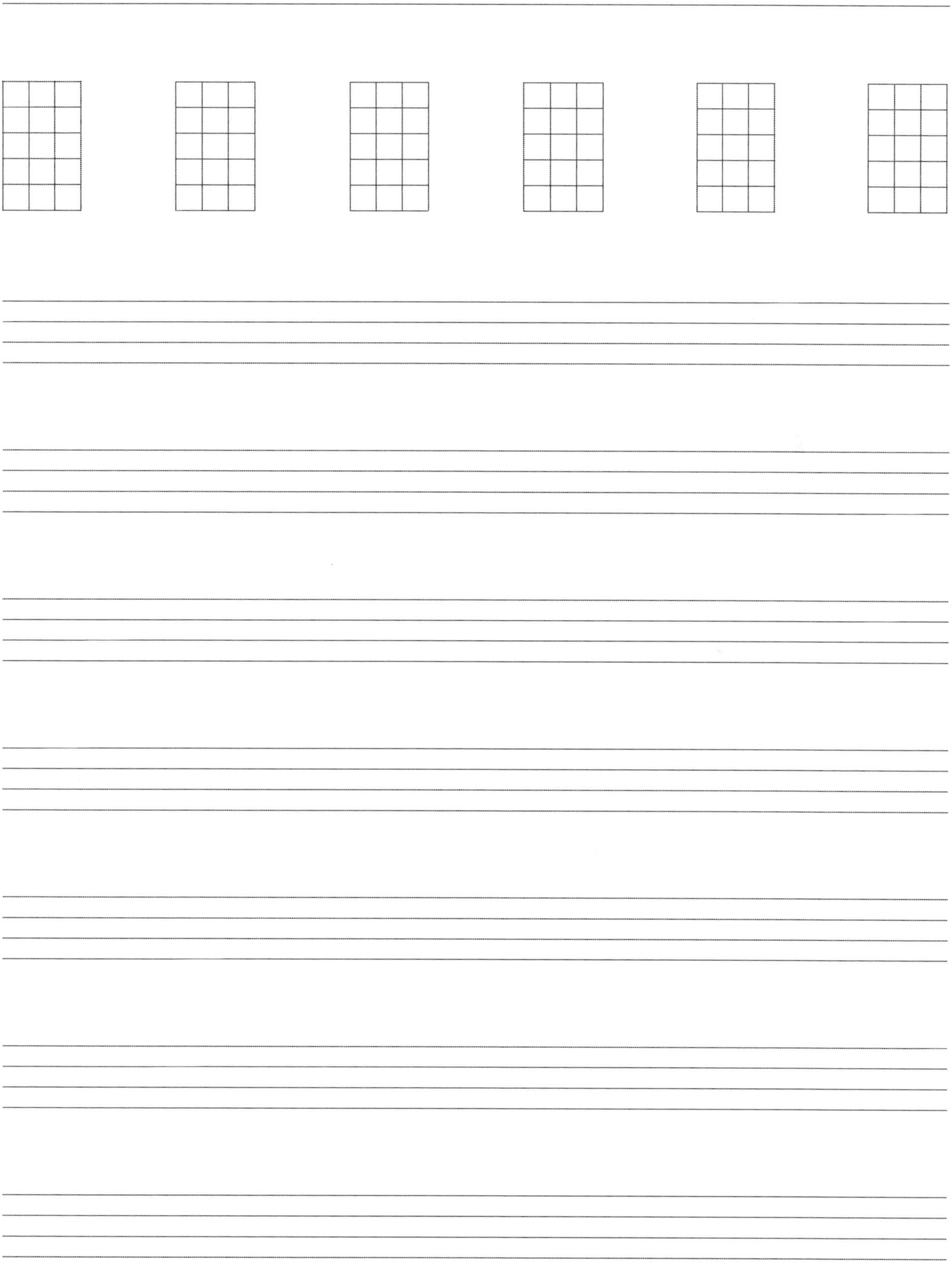

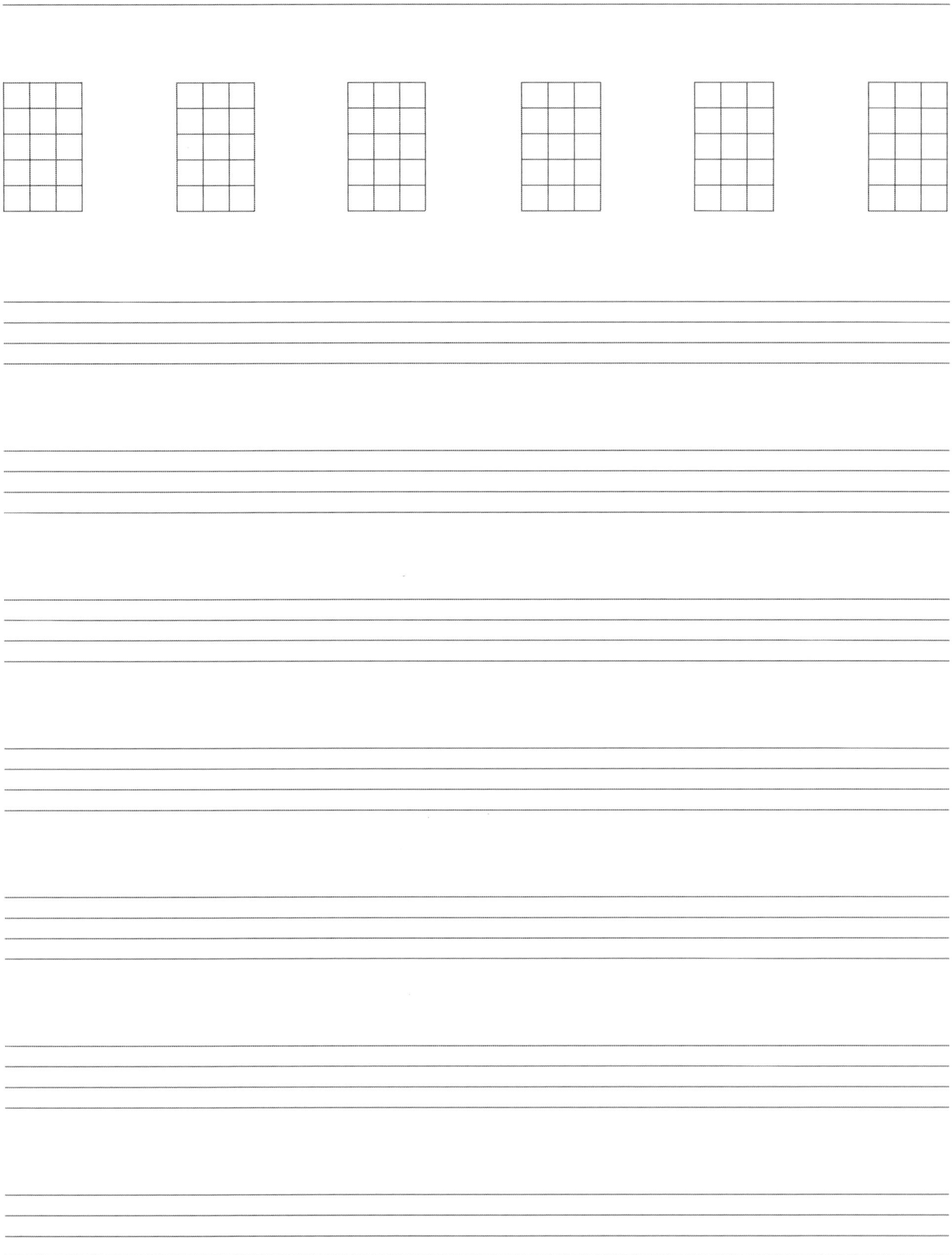

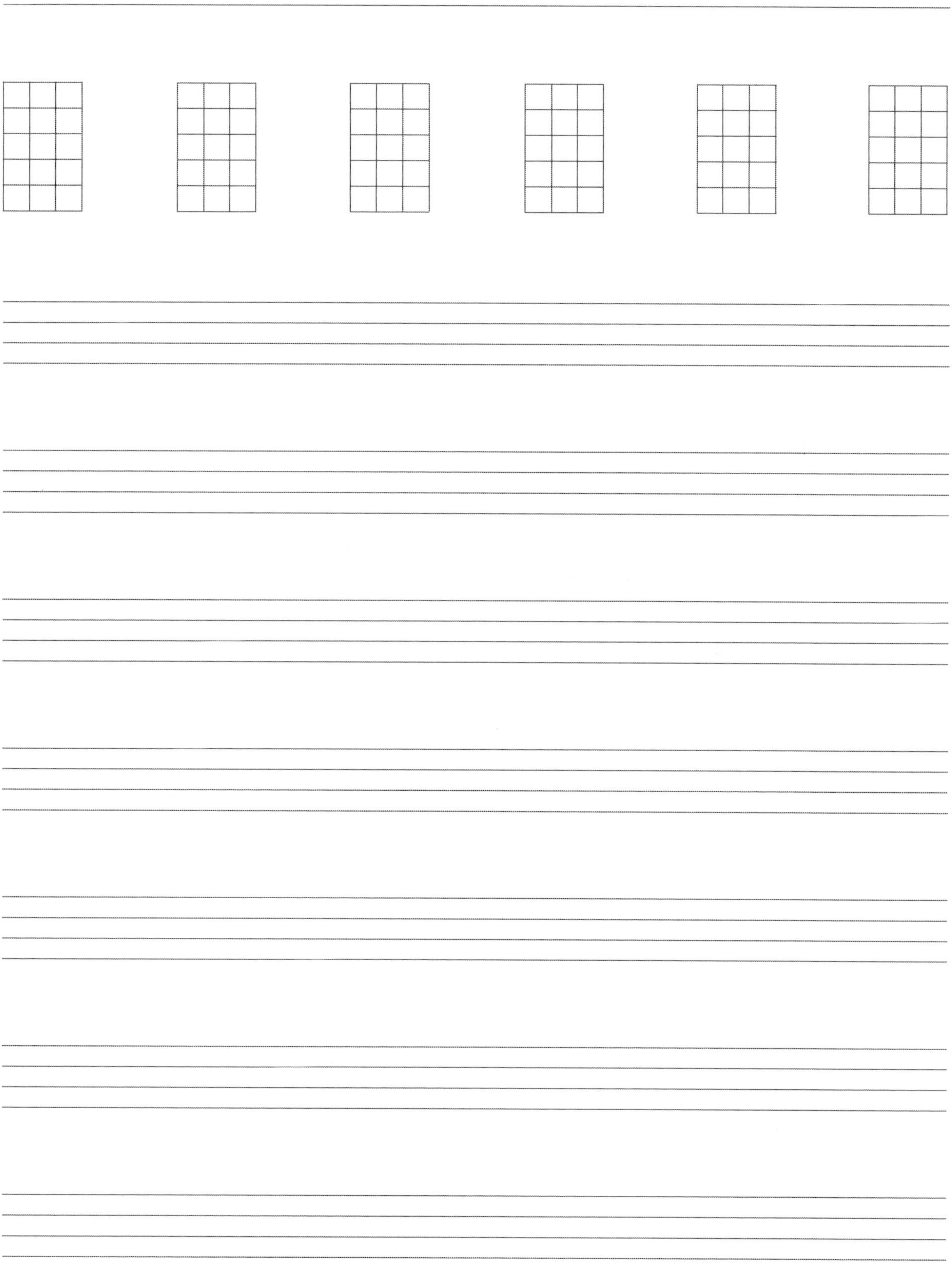

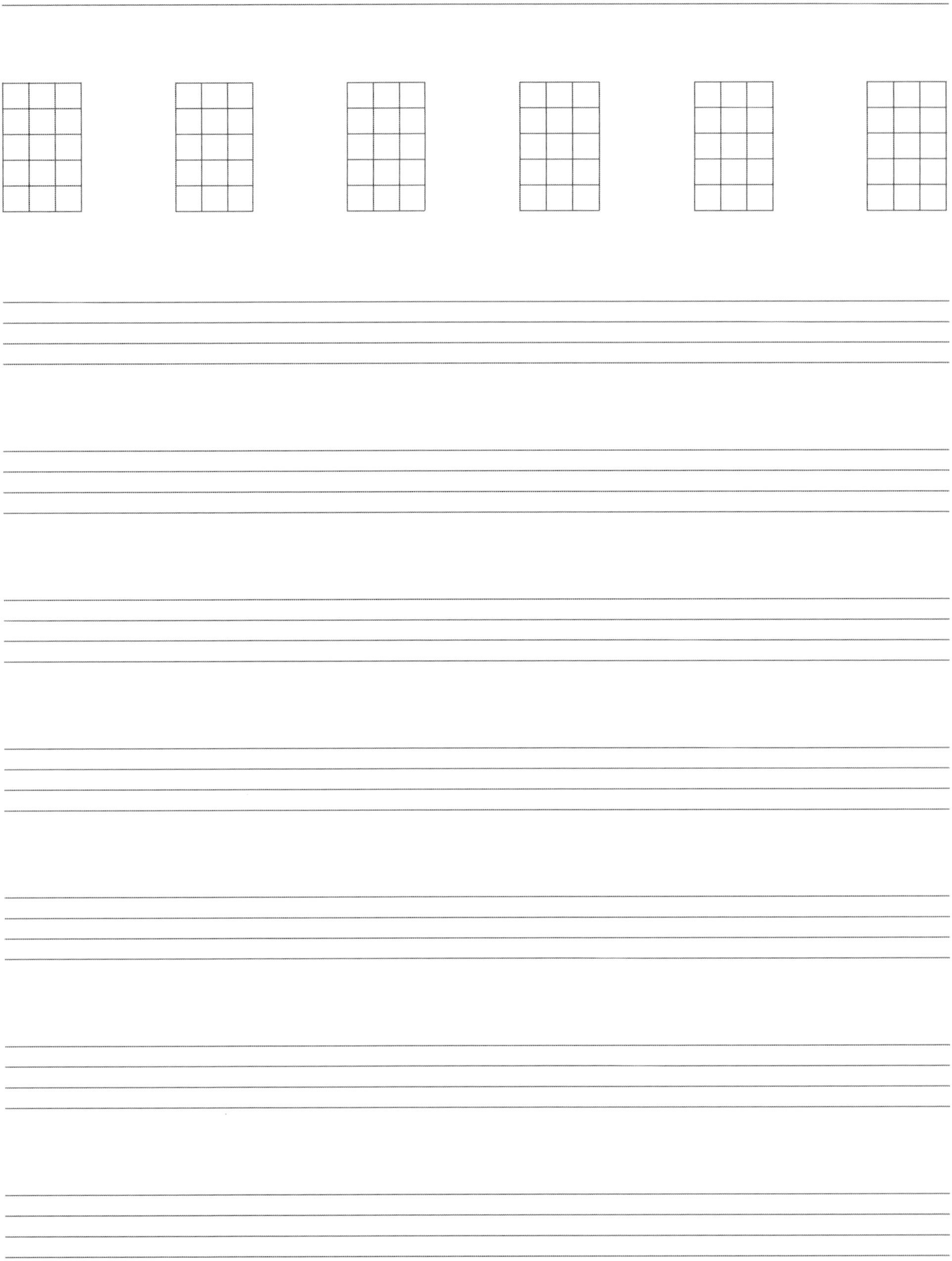

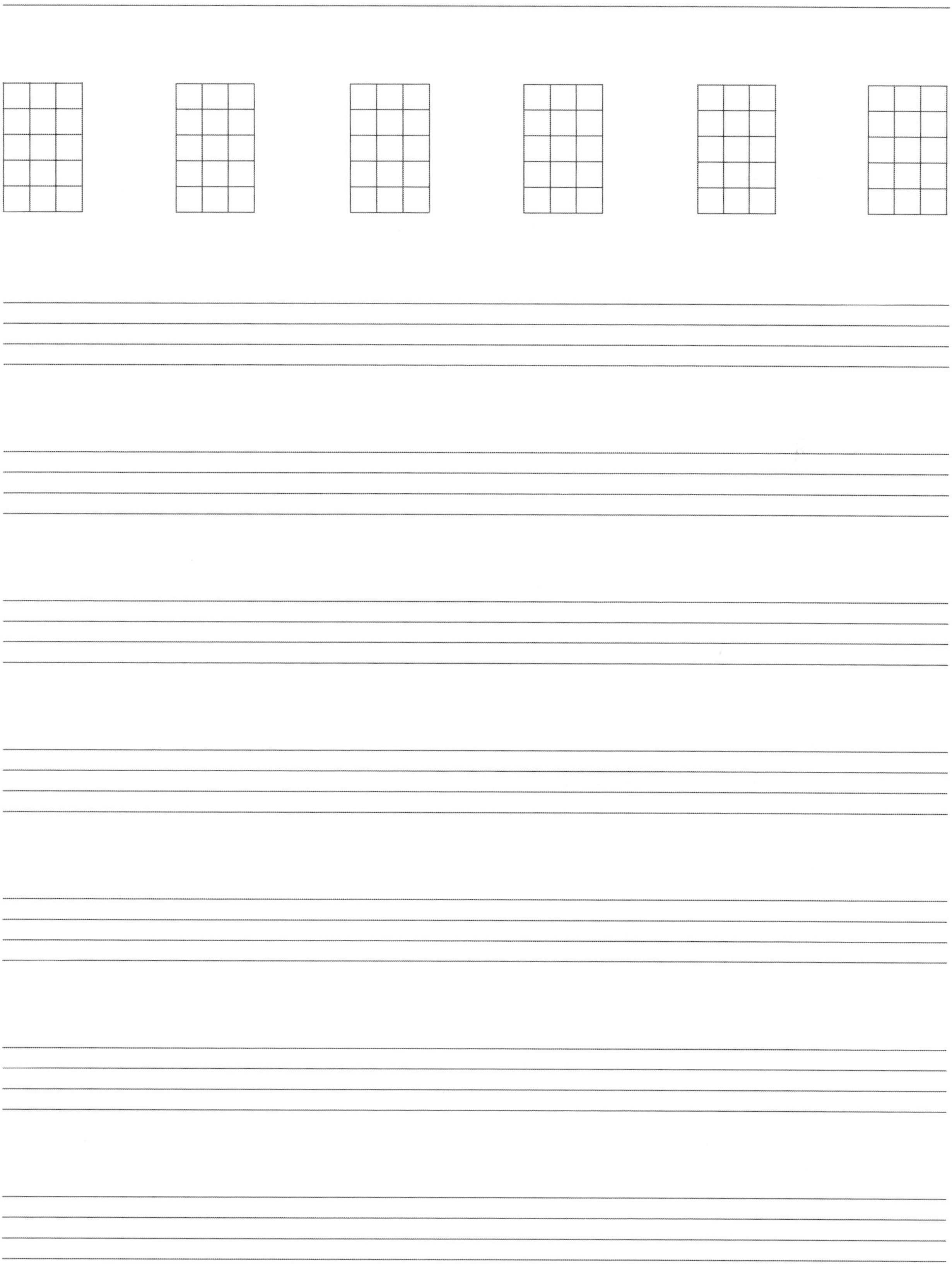

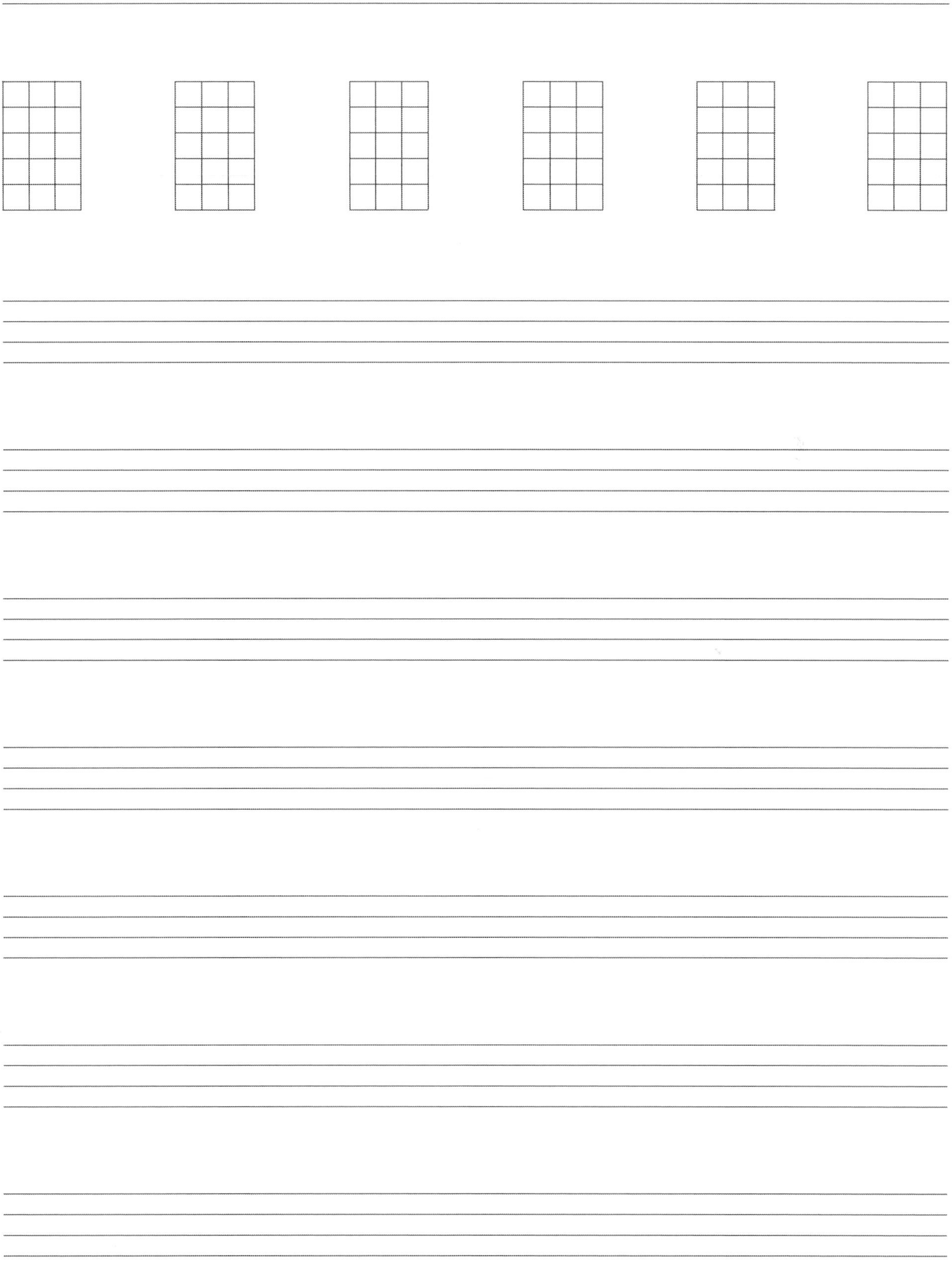

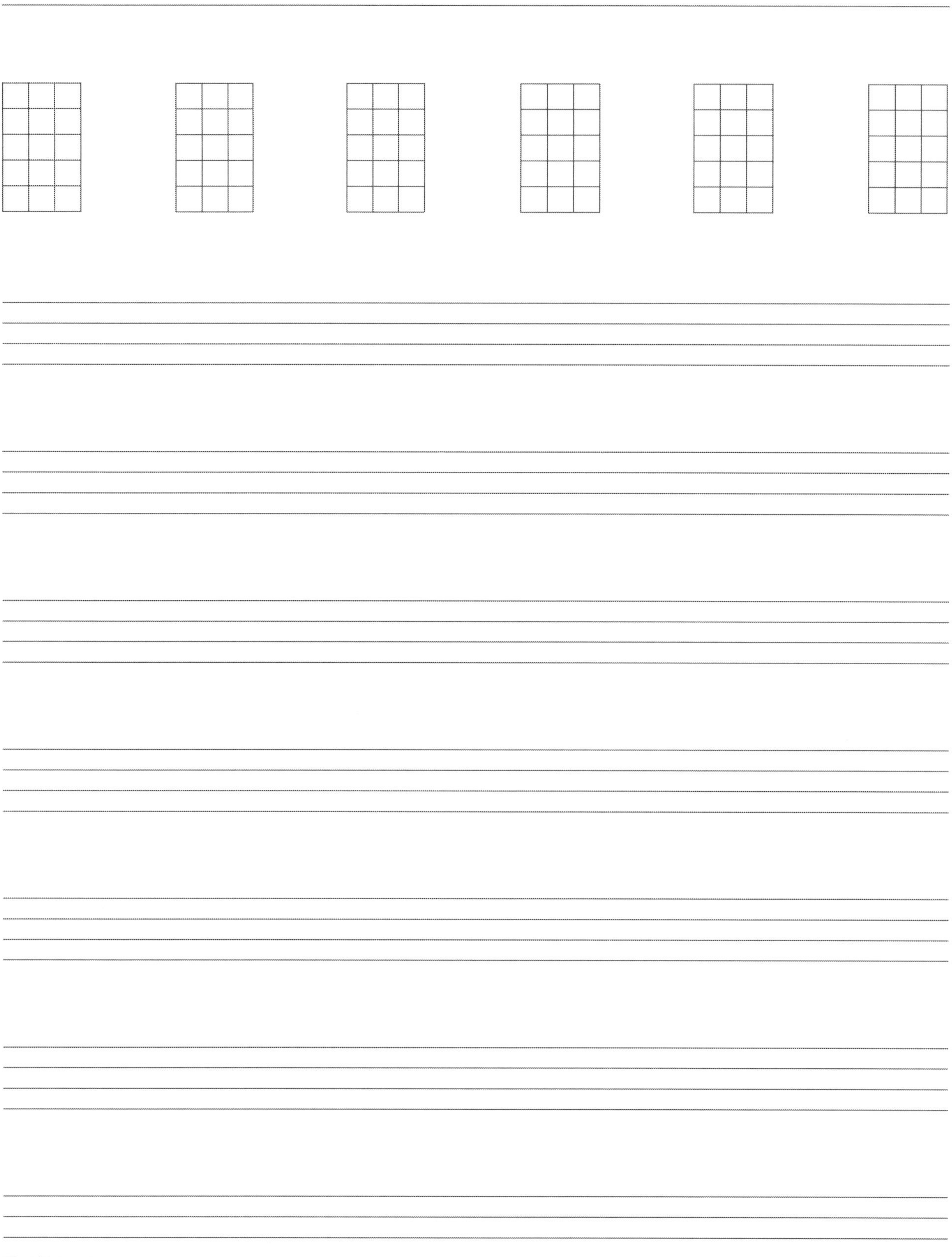

Made in the USA
Columbia, SC
02 December 2020

26119509R00057